The Skin Cancer Information Handbook

By Michael D. Miller

> **Every single person who has cancer has a pH that is too acidic.**
>
> Dr. Otto Warburg won the Nobel Prize in 1931 for proving that cancer can't survive in an alkaline, oxygen rich environment but thrives in an acidic, low oxygen environment.

Quote by Dr. Otto Warburg, Nobel Prize Winner

{Author Announcement If you have a serious case of skin cancer, you may not have time to read this book before you treat your malignancy. Therefore, in such a case, we suggest that you go directly to our instructions on how to make and use our "Super Dooper Skin Cancer Salve".

 So Please go to Page 44 where we will tell you how to make and use our wonder salve. You can read the rest of the book later.}

Table of Contents:

Chapter		Page
Foreword		
Chapter 1	Background	4
Chapter 2	How Cancer begins	13
Chapter 3	About Acids	17
Chapter 4	Alkalinity Blood	25
Chapter 5	Parasite Connection	29
Chapter 6	Your Fat	35
Chapter 7	Solutions	41
Chapter 8	Our Special Salve	44
Chapter 9	My Ephipany	49
Chapter 10	Conclusion	59
Chapter 11	Alternative Cancer	66

Chapter One

Before We Begin:

Penicillin (our first antibiotic) was discovered in 1893. But it was not used until 1943, when the many medical emergencies of WWII caused it to be tried. So how was it that we were denied the use of this fantastic medicine for 50 years? How many people were in pain or died unnecessarily during those 50 years who could have been saved by antibiotics?

The answer to why it was not used for 50 years is that it took 50 years for the mainstream medical establishment to begin to believe that it worked. It took 50 years for this new knowledge to work itself through the medical system.

It is important to remember this story about penicillin as you read this booklet. For we believe that the information in this booklet is also 50 years ahead of its time. The mainstream medical establishment is just now beginning to ponder on the possibility that most degenerative diseases and many of the causes of aging are caused by acid deposits in the body. It doesn't even begin to state what may be causing these toxic deposits to form there.

We don't have 50 years to wait for their enlightenment. So plunge in, read this booklet and get 50 years (at least) ahead of the system.

My Approach

Many years ago, when I was a young man in the army, I attended a lot of classes presented by young noncommissioned officers (sergeants). They did a good job in teaching us about weapons, equipment, tactics, etc., especially given their own limited experience in teaching in a public forum.

The army had given them good training in how to do this. Part of this training concerned using the proper format to use when teaching new information. Basically, the format that they used was, quite simply:

1. The Introduction. "Tell them what you are going to teach them".

2. The Presentation. "Tell them what they need to know".
3. The Summary. "Tell them what you told them".

So now, these many years later, I fondly remember these experiences. And I am going to use the same format now to make my presentation to you. So here goes.

"The Introduction"

In this book, "The Skin Cancer Information Handbook", I am going to show you:

1. How a doctor by the name of Otto Warburg, way back in 1934, discovered that cancer was caused by a lack of oxygen in the body. He was awarded the Nobel Prize for his discovery.

2. How a research doctor from Australia named Robert O. Young discovered that overacidification (too much acid) of the body led to the amounts of oxygen in the body to be reduced to

the dangerous point where lack of oxygenation in the body led to grown of the cancer virus in the body.

3. How Dr. Robert O. Young discovered that when the oxygen levels in the body drop to below 50% of normal levels, an anerobic (lack of oxygen) condition exists where the cancer virus (which is anerobic, and thrives in an oxygen starved environment) will begin to grow and thrive.

4. The eventual result is cancer.

5. Holistic medical researchers have also discovered that there are ready and efficient methods to reduce the acidification of the body back to a healthy point, a point where cancer viruses cannot thrive. One of these methods is Hydrogen Peroxide Therapy.

6. Skin Cancer is a form of cancer where the actual cancer growth appears on the external surface of the body. This

presents an excellent and easy to apply opportunity for hydrogen peroxide therapy.

7. It has been discovered that a thin paste of 35% food grade hydrogen peroxide, mixed with a "sticking agent" such as aloe vera gel, when applied topically to the surface of the skin where the skin cancer is located will bombard the anerobic cancer cells with oxygen, thus killing the skin cnacer growth.

8. We are going to show you how to make this "Sooper Dooper Healing Salve'.

9. WaaLa! No more skin cancer.

Now let's take a look at the Presentation

"The Presentation"

Chapter Two

Background and Overview

(Our Message In a Nutshell)

When I was 62 years old I had arthritis. For 7 years my body had slowly stiffened up. I had reached the point that I could not pick up anything that fell on the floor. That was a frustrating feeling. Plus, many normal recreational and hobby pursuits were no longer possible. Heck, I could not even put on my socks without pain.

I have an avid interest in holistic medicine and natural healing. So for years I have read everything that I could find about arthritis and associated diseases such as diabetes. I tried numerous remedies. My research on the interactions of the human body that cause such affliction became an insatiable quest. I learned why arthritis and diabetes are more common today than ever before. Then I found the solution.

As with many great truths, the secret of how I cured my illness is very simple. And I learned that my holistic solution is also the solution for some 150 other degenerative diseases, including obesity and diabetes. It will also be the solution for many of the other afflictions that are associated with aging. Once you read and understand my discovery, you will understand that it will probably resolve your health problems. It also will help you to maintain your energy and overall vigor.

But first I have to explain some basic things about how your body works.

Each individual cell of your body is an independent organism. It needs to be fed oxygen and food in order to live and prosper, and it also produces waste products that have to be removed from the cell for it to remain healthy.

It is the job of your blood to perform these functions. Your blood carries fresh oxygen and food to each cell of your body, and then having completed this task, it picks up the waste products (also called toxins) from the cell. These waste products are carried by the blood to the walls of your intestines. There the waste products (toxins) are passed through the walls of the intestine, to be excreted from your body along with your body's food waste products.

That is how it is supposed to work, and that is how it works for most of us during our younger years. But as we age, things begin to change.

Your Body's *ph* Balance

Now let's talk about your body's acid/alkaline balance (also know as *ph*). Every farmer and agronomist will tell you that plants grow best in soils that have the proper *ph* for that plant. That is because every organism has a range of alkalinity/acidity in which it will prosper. Outside of that range of *ph,* the organism dies or is greatly stressed just to survive. Thus it is that corn will not grow well in soil that is too alkaline, and carrots will not grow well in soil that is too acidic.

Our bodies are the same. There is a range of acidity/alkalinity for our bodies in which they function perfectly. But should the body's acidity/alkalinity balance fall outside of this range, the body becomes stressed, its ability to function properly becomes decreased, and eventually this stressed condition will lead to a degenerative disease that may eventually cause death.

In today's world, there is a strong tendency for our bodies to become too acidic. That is because we eat too much acidic food. Red meats are highly acidic, as is soda pop, most processed food, and fried foods. Even carbohydrates and sugars turn acidic during the digestion process.

How many years has it been since my high school physics teacher soaked a dried chicken leg bone in a glass of coca cola? Within an hour the bone could be tied into a knot because of the acidity of the cola. But we tend to ignore all this. Thus it is that our bodies slowly tend to become acidic. It is a slow process, and we don't notice it.

That is okay when we are in our twenties and thirties. But by the time we reach our forties, fifties and sixties, the accumulated effect of eating too much acidic food begins to show up as pain, and our bodies become dangerously acidic.

Lets talk specifics here. At a *ph* of 7.2, the body is in perfect *ph* balance, neither too acidic or too alkaline. A *ph* range of 7.0 to 7.5 is the acceptable range for a body to be in good health. When the *ph* drops to between 6.5 and 7.0, the body is beginning to get stressed and fatigue and a feeling of pain or lethargy begins to set in. When the *ph* drops to between 6.0 and 6.5, the body is beginning to become seriously acidic, and it is probably developing one or more of the 150 specific degenerative diseases or pains that are associated with an acetic condition. Then when your *ph* gets to between 6.0 and 5.5, you are in serious trouble, your energy levels are shot, and a degenerative disease or pain of some sort is upon you.

When I discovered this very simple but crucial bit of information, I checked my *ph*. It was 5.5. No wonder I was having health problems!

Chapter Two

How Degenerative Disease (Including Arthritis and Cancer) Begins

Now lets talk about how this situation leads to degenerative diseases.

Okay, you have led a good life, used moderation in most things, and have good health. But gradually, unknown to you, your body acidity has slowly, over the years, increased. As your acidity has increased, your body has experienced several reactions to this changed condition. A general feeling of fatigue and tiredness has set in. But also, the acidic condition of your blood now affects its ability to perform a function that it used to perform with ease. The ability of your stressed blood to carry food and oxygen to the body's cells, and its ability to carry away the waste products from the cells is lessened.

Your blood, now unable to easily perform these functions, becomes overloaded with waste products (toxins) that it cannot easily dispose of. So it looks for other ways to dispose of the waste products. Some of them it stores in your fat deposits. Others it stores as deposits in the linings of your veins and arteries, or in your pancreas. And others it deposits on places where your bones are exposed, such as the bone joints of your body.

It is these deposits of certain toxins (waste products) in your bone joints that eventually manifest as degenerative disease. The deposits of toxins that accumulate in your pancreas will cause diabetes. Acids and toxins in your blood cause your body to produce cholesterol to protect the lining of your arteries. This leads to high blood pressure and heart disease. Lowered oxygen leads to cancer.

So, as I have outlined here, my illness was in actuality caused by a long-term over-acidity in my body. Once I realized this, I began to look for a direct and simple treatment to change my *ph* balance (acidy/alkalinity) back to a healthy range. Eventually I found a blend of mineral compounds and herbs that gave me pain relief, leading to total symptom reversal.

After I began treatment, my recovery was dramatic. Within 6 weeks of treatment my *ph* had gone from 5.5 to 6.5. Not only did my pain and other symptoms begin to disappear, I also regained much of my prior energy and zest for life. Now my acidity levels are in the healthy range, and it is easy for me to keep them that way. What I especially like is that no draconian diet changes were necessary.

You think to yourself, "I would rather be dead than follow this diet!". No beef, no bread, no potatoes, no seafood, no cheese? Yes, the above type of alkalizing diet is too stringent for most of us. So what else can we do? Well that is the purpose of this booklet; to explain to you a much simpler way to reduce the acid levels in your body down to a healthy level so that your health problems go away.

"NO disease, including cancer, can exist in an alkaline environment."

- Dr. Otto Warburg- 1931 Nobel Prize winner for cancer discovery.

Dr. Otto Warburg

Chapter Three

More About Acids in Your Body

The concept that an acid/alkaline imbalance in the body is a major cause of disease isn't new. Remember Edgar Cayce, the famous sleeping prophet from back in the 1930s and 1940s? He often suggested body detoxification, colonics, fasting, massage, steam baths and alkalizing the body by diet modification (see our addendum). He also on occasion recommended ingesting baking soda as a remedy for overacidity.

Back in 1933 Dr. William Howard published a breakthrough book titled *A New Health Era* in which he postulated that self-poisoning by acid accumulation in the body was a major cause of all illnesses. He stated, "We depart from health in the proportion to which we have allowed our alkalis to be dissipated by the introduction of too much acid forming food. It may seem strange to say, but all disease is the same thing, no matter what its form of expression, but it is so."

As we presently live, very few of us can rid our bodies of all the acids that we create from stress, foods, and our metabolisms. These acid wastes move around the body via the blood and lymphatic system until they reach our kidneys. Our kidneys are many times overloaded with toxin accumulation, so that they cannot process the new waste. Our blood and lymphatic fluid, unable to dispose of the acid waste in the kidneys, seeks an alternative way to get rid of the waste. They must do this so that they can resume their main job of carrying oxygen and nutrients t the cells of the body. So the blood and lymphatic fluid take an alternate route; they dispose of the acid waste by dumping it into our fat, veins, organs, or bone joints (the resulting deposits thus causing arthritis) or the pancreas (resulting in diabetes). Both cholesterol and crystallized uric acid are formed from the "dumped" acid wastes that could not be processed by the kidneys.

Harmful Effects of Acid

Acid coagulates blood. Also blood has problems flowing around fatty acids, and thus tends to clump. Capillaries then clog up and die. The skin, deprived of life-giving blood, loses elasticity and begins to wrinkle. We begin to look old.

It is not only your skin. Without a proper acid/alkaline balance, every part of the body works harder to maintain health. All systems (lungs, organs, skin, etc.) work to and depend on the maintenance of a correct blood pH. Your organs and cells are totally subservient to your blood and the blood acid level (pH). All organs work to keep your blood at a balanced pH, to the point where your body is willing to inflict major damages on other parts of your body that stand in the way of a correct blood pH. In other words, your body will damage itself in order to keep a proper blood pH. This is because if the blood pH strays out of a very narrow range, you will die.

The Proper PH Level:

If your blood pH dips from its optimal pH of 7.2 down to lower levels (indicating an acidity condition) your health will be affected. Especially important is that the ability of your blood to carry oxygen to the cells of your body will be lessened.! The proper blood pH is that critical!

So your body knows what it doing when it disposes of acid wastes in a manner that eventually causes you illness and pain.

One of the reasons that you get a charge from drinking a cola (pH of 2.5, very acidic) is that this acidity sets off alarm bells all over your body. The resulting surge of adrenaline gives you the rush that you get from the cola.

Dr. Robert O. Young

Alkaline chemicals that are stored in your body rush to neutralize the acids. This deprives the rest of your body of these alkalizing chemicals (such as calcium in your bones).

About Stress: Of all the acidifying factors, stress is the greatest. Stress can neutralize and acidify an alkaline diet with just one surge of adrenaline.

This is important. We can show you how to reduce the acid levels in your body to a healthy level, but you must also work hard to keep the stress low in your life. If there is unavoidable stress, learn to control it or to channel it so that its effect on you is minimized.

Long Term Effects of Acidity

We have 60,000 miles of veins and arteries in our bodies. Acids eat into and corrode these veins and arteries. If left unchecked, it eventually interrupts or damages all cellular activity and function, to even include the beating of our heart to the nerve functions within our brain.

In addition, if the blood cells are so loaded with toxins that they cannot dispose of, the blood cells cannot carry enough oxygen back to the body cells to meet their oxygen needs. Thus the body's cells get starved for oxygen. This is really catastrophic. Without sufficient oxygen, the cells get stressed, then weaken, then age prematurely, then die.

Incredibly, Dr. Otto Warburg in 1934 was awarded the Nobel Prize for discovering that cancer was caused by a lack of oxygen in the body cells. He found that when the oxygen level of your blood falls below 50 percent of normal, an anaerobic condition is created in which cancer can prosper [anaerobic means "absence of oxygen"].

Dr. Otto Warburg

It actually is quite simple. The cancer virus is anaerobic; that is, it can only live in an absence of oxygen. Cancer cells exposed to oxygen will die. An obvious solution for cancer, and many other illnesses (including AIDS) is to maintain oxygen levels in the body above the 50 percent level.

Why the mainstream medical establishment has ignored these facts for some seventy years is interesting. I will leave it to you to ponder on this.

In summary, over-acidity damages life itself, leading to all forms of sickness and disease, as well as general symptoms of aging. As you are probably beginning to realize, this story is just not about a certain disease and how to cure it, it is also about explaining to you one of the principal causes of disease and aging, and telling you how to correct the matter. This is powerful stuff. If you are like me, you will eventually be thankful for this knowledge.

Dr. Theo Barody

You will appreciate this for having opened up your knowledge and awareness so that you can maintain a much healthier body and lead a much longer and healthier life.

Without good health, we have nothing!

In his book, *Alkalize or Die*, Dr. Theodore A. Baroody, MD states, "Too much acidity in the body is like having too little oil in the car. It just grinds to a halt one day and dies. There you are-stuck. The body also does the same thing. It starts painfully creaking to a stop along the byways of life and you find yourself in some kind of discomfort. I watch with great concern as people of all classes and lifestyles suffer from this excess."

He attributes 68 major health conditions (including cancer, of course) to acidic conditions in the body. His book is great to read, and I highly recommend it.

Chapter Four:

All about Alkalinity and Blood

Your blood is meant to always be slightly alkaline. It must be slightly alkaline in order to maintain resistance to decay and the possible growth of bad or harmful organisms that can grow in an acidic environment. Therefore the blood has a very narrow range of pH in which it can operate. As we have previously (somewhat dramatically, for effect!) stated, if your blood gets outside of this acceptable range of pH, you will die.

The absolutely perfect pH level of your blood is 7.365. The pH level is that exact.

If the blood gets slightly outside this pH level, results will be felt in every part of your body. Harmful and poisoning organisms that can grow and multiply in an acidic environment begin to do so. They take on the function of aggressive, parasitic and pathogenic agents (a hint here for candida suffers of why you have a yeast infection in your body that does not go away).

Scientists and researchers can use a dark field microscope to see the changes in the blood that take place as blood acidity increases. They watch the repetitive pattern unfolding as disease organisms proliferate and grow, and they document the ensuing debilitation of the body that, if left unchecked, will eventually kill us, one way or another.

The Power of pH

The pH scale is logarithmic. This means that each pH value is ten times higher than the previous number. For example, if your pH goes from 7 to 6, it means that your body is **ten times** more acidic. This is very important to understand as you begin to monitor your blood acidity levels.

Your goal should be to maintain a body pH level of somewhere around 7. I am able to eat whatever I want and still maintain a pH level of from 6.6 to 7.0 by using the practices that this book will explain. This keeps me happy, I feel great, and I live with the knowledge that many diseases, such as cancer, etc, will have a hard time living in my body. All this, in addition to the fact that my arthritis has gone away!

A glass of cola has a pH of 2.5 (very acidic). It is approximately 50,000 times more acidic than a glass of water! One of the active ingredients in cola is phosphoric acid. Not to beat up too much on colas, but when I was in a high school science class (a long time ago), my teacher conducted an experiment. He placed a dried-out chicken drumstick bone in a container of cola. After only 30 minutes he removed the previously dried out and rigid chicken leg bone from the cola, and he then tied it into a knot. The cola had softened the bone that much! All this to demonstrate to us the acidity of colas. I guess that I wasn't too impressed, because I kept right on drinking colas until just a few years ago when my overacidity caused me to wise up in this matter. Now I drink bottled diet iced tea from the vending machines.

I consider a body pH level of 7.0 to be good. Conversely, if your blood pH level dropped to 7.0 you would die. It would mean that your blood (with an ideal level of ph 7.365) had become almost four times too acidic. You would then die from blood poisoning. All this is to explain to you that the rest of your body is totally committed to maintaining your blood at the correct pH, and the rest of your body will sacrifice itself totally (including giving itself arthritis, (for example) in order to protect the pH level of your blood.

I hope that I have explained this satisfactorily. Whereas your body can and does function at a wide range of pH (basically from 7.2 to 5.5), your blood does not. Your body knows this, and does everything possible to protect the blood pH. This protection includes sacrificing other body functions and parts in order to protect the blood. So your disease is part of your body's efforts to protect the pH level of your blood. Your body, believe it or not, knew what it was doing when it gave you an illness or made you fat!

Chapter Five

The Alkalinity and Parasite Connection

As we have explained, acidity in your body permits disease organisms to grow and thrive. This includes simple germs, yeasts, fungi, viruses and molds. These microorganisms all produce excretions (excrement). These excretions are toxic to your body. The organisms not only eat glucose, fats and protein from our bodies, they also poison our bodies with the resulting excretions. In short, they take our food and turn it into poison.

Again, the symptoms of this parasite poisoning may not be patently obvious, but they are there. They manifest as the gradual weakening of our bodies that we otherwise attribute to aging, tiredness, overwork, etc.

It is kind of like when a lumberjack cuts down a big tree with his axe. It takes many whacks from the axe before the tree falls, each small whack removing a tiny portion of the tree. But the tree does eventually fall, the cumulative effects of the many small whacks taking their effect. Well, consider the parasite poisoning in your body as one of those small whacks.

Dr. Robert O. Young

You will appreciate this for having opened up your knowledge and awareness so that you can maintain a much healthier body and lead a much longer and healthier life. **Without good health, we have nothing!**

Watch out, or eventually you will also, as did the big tree, fall and die. Get rid of those parasites now by balancing the pH levels in your body. Get rid of your acidity!

Alkalinity and Minerals

As you know, minerals are essential to your health. Properly assimilating the minerals into your body is also important. Many of you have read how much of the nutritive value of the mineral supplements that we take is lost to us because our bodies do not properly assimilate the minerals in their supplement form.

Each mineral has its own special "signature" pH level that it needs in order to be assimilated into your body. This is critical to understand. I repeat: each mineral has its own special "signature" pH level that it needs in order to be assimilated into your body.

Every chemistry classroom has a chart of periodic elements, including all minerals. Those minerals at the lower end are capable of being assimilated in the body over a broader range of body pH. Those higher on the chart require a much narrower range of pH in order to be assimilated. In short, if your body is too acidic your body will simply reject many minerals that are critical to your health.

One example of why this is important: Look at iodine. It is high on the periodic scale, and therefore requires almost perfect pH levels in the body in order to be assimilated. Iodine is required for a healthy thyroid. If our body is too acidic, the thyroid will receive insufficient iodine, and thus cannot perform properly. A malfunctioning thyroid is connected to arthritis, cancer, diabetes, heart attacks depression, fatigue and obesity. Yet few of us are able to connect the dots and recognize that these illnesses are caused by your malfunctioning thyroid, which is caused by overacidity. Interesting, is it not? Tragic, is it not?

This mineral assimilation situation is made worse because our agricultural lands have become mineral depleted. Overuse of chemical fertilizers (that only provide three of the eight-two necessary minerals and trace elements that our bodies need) and overuse of insecticides and pesticides have caused our soils to not provide our fruits and vegetables with the minerals that we need. It has been shown that today's vegetables only provide 25% of the mineral nutrition that they provided 70 years ago (before the introduction of chemical fertilizers after WWII.). This in itself is an interesting story, too long to tell here. But it bears merit for further study on your part. Lets fix your health problems first!

Dr. W.R. Kellas

As you begin to de-acidify your body, you may experience a variety of detoxification symptoms such as headaches, body pains and aches, stiffness, itching, etc. These signs are often referred to as a "healing crisis" and they are your body's way of telling you that it is being changed (for the better).

Chapter Six

Is Your Fat Saving Your Life?

Many of us suffer the pains and arrows of outrageous fortune due to obesity. Yes. Fat is a major problem in today's world. But it is not just that we eat too much or that we eat the wrong foods. Believe it or not, overacidity in our bodies also causes us to be fat. This explains why many of us (myself included) do not respond satisfactorily to diet and exercise. We fast and work out, and the fat still doesn't come off. What gives?

Our bodies actually resist giving up the fat because the fat is actually saving our lives. Is this a wild statement or what?

Why Our Bodies Cling To Their Fat

Dr. Lynda Frassetto, MD, from the University of California has researched this matter. She believes that humans, in evolutionary terms, have changed. Once upon a time, our bodies used to break down food and dispose of the acid waste with our kidneys and livers. But now, because of the sheer amount of acid waste the average American produces, she sees our inner bodies being turned into a war zone, where our body is fighting to protect its most strategic reserves --- our kidney and liver -- from total degradation and failure.

One of the ways that our body does this is by finding somewhere else to store the body waste products (including crystallized uric acid). May times this somewhere else is the fatty deposits. So, as far as your body is concerned, you fat is important to it because it has your waste toxins stored there.

You exercise and diet in order to make your fat go away. But your body says to itself, "I need that Fat. That is my warehouse for stored toxins." So it holds onto the fat. It resists losing weight. And you get frustrated because you remain fat because you do not understand the real problem. The real problem is overacidity in your body. We seem a bit redundant here, don't we? But it is important for you to appreciate this wisdom and knowledge. In actuality, your body thinks that it is saving your life by clinging onto that fat!

An Evolutionary Change

(Author's Note) Some of this info provided by Dr. Frassetto below repeats information that we have already covered. But a bit of redundancy here may be in order, as this information is so darn important!

To prove this theory, Dr. Frassetto studied 1000 people and discovered that we are indeed stockpiling acid waste in our fatty deposits instead of eliminating it with our kidneys and liver. Cholesterol and crystallized uric acid are solidified acids that have been dumped within the body for later disposal, which never comes. Our bodies have made the choice to preserve our kidney and liver instead of processing the acid waste. The cost is tremendous -- obesity, low energy, and many acid related diseases such as arthritis, diabetes, cancer, painful periods, and much more.

When our bodies are excessively acidic, they borrow essential minerals such as calcium, sodium, potassium, and magnesium from our vital organs and bones to buffer or neutralize the acid. The result is our bodies suffer from prolonged degradation or corrosion, which manifests into these dehabilitating conditions and pains.

The reason is simple -- the average American diet contains way too much acid. Diet coke and other soda is probably the most acidic food people consume at a pH of 2.5. Beer and meat are at 3.5, then there's dairy, white pasta, most water, wine, hard alcohol, nuts and butters, beans, oils -- all acidic foods. All produce acid waste in our bodies that they can't handle. Dr. Robert O. Young agrees with Dr. Frassetto's theory. Sugar is an acid and she sees Westerners consumption of sugar as the reason why so many are overweight. The body has to protect itself from the excess sugar, so it creates fat to encase the acid. "Fat," she says. "Is saving our lives."

Then there's the problem of disease. The stomach works by producing acid to break down food. Whenever this acid is made, alkaline buffers are also created and sent through our blood stream, naturally alkalizing our body. A healthy balanced body has alkaline reserves to battle diseases, infections, and viruses. But if excessive acid must be continuously neutralized or stored, our alkaline reserves will be depleted, leaving our bodies weakened and disease prone.

Acid and Stress

Dr. Frassetto says that acid comes from three sources -- food, pollution, and stress. Of these three, stress is the greatest problem. One shot of adrenaline can neutralize and acidify an alkaline diet. So stress management as well as diet management is essential to maintaining an alkaline body that is free of pain.

She says that the worst case scenario in which many Westerners fit into is where we work 40-50 hour stressful weeks with hardly any breaks to calm ourselves down. We consume fast food and coffee for quick bursts of artificial energy to just get through our workday. Then we come home to family stresses, household chores, bills, and more and never really relax and give our bodies a chance to neutralize all the acid we produced through stress and from eating very acidic
foods. So acid in our bodies build up until we begin to show symptoms -- digestive problems, headaches, overweight, bone

pains, elimination issues, muscle tension and pain, heart problems, high blood pressure, and more. We spend our lives giving ourselves to our jobs and families and never take the time to nourish our bodies, mind, and soul.

More Effects of Acid on our Body

Dr. Frassetto also says that acidity is like rust. Our veins and arteries are corroded by acid. If nothing is done, acid interrupts all cellular activities and functions -- from our beating heart to the way we think. Blood also can't flow around fatty acids so capillaries clog up and die. Our skin begins to wrinkle and isn't as stretchy. Pains develop. Even if you put out the money for a face-lift or liposuction, the acid still remains and will do damage. As for our lungs and other organs, all are involved in the maintenance of correct blood pH so if all have to work harder to deal with excessive acid, all will stop functioning a whole lot sooner than we want them to. Did you know that if any substance changes from a 7 to an 8 pH, it has become ten times more alkaline? The opposite is also true, if it changes from a 7 pH to a 6, it has become ten times more acidic.

Chapter Seven

Lets Talk About Solutions for Skin cancer!

Our Solution for Skin Cancer!

Okay now that we have pretty thoroughly explained about body acidity and your health, and how body acidity affects the oxygen levels of your body, let's talk about our fool-proof solution for skin cancer. Let's review what we have proposed:

1. We discussed how a doctor by the name of Otto Warburg, way back in 1931, discovered that cancer was caused by a lack of oxygen in the body. He was awarded the Nobel Prize for his discovery.

2. We discussed how a research doctor from Australia named Robert O. Young discovered that overacidification (too much acid) of the body led to the amounts of oxygen in the body to be reduced to the dangerous point where lack of oxygenation in the body led to grown of the cancer virus in the body.

3. How Dr. Robert O. Young discovered that when the oxygen levels in the body drop to below 50% of normal levels, an anerobic (lack of oxygen) condition exists where the cancer virus (which is anerobic, and thrives in an oxygen starved environment) will begin to grow and thrive.

4. The eventual result is cancer.

5. Holistic medical researchers have also discovered that there are ready and efficient methods to reduce the acidification of the body back to a healthy point, a point where cancer

viruses cannot thrive. One of these methods is Hydrogen Peroxide Therapy.

6. Skin Cancer is a form of cancer where the actual cancer growth appears on the external surface of the body. This presents an excellent and easy to apply opportunity for hydrogen peroxide therapy.

7. **It has been discovered that a thin paste of 35% food grade hydrogen peroxide, mixed with a "sticking agent" such as aloe vera gel, when applied topically to the surface of the skin where the skin cancer is located will bombard the anerobic cancer cells with oxygen, thus killing the skin cnacer growth.**

8. Waala! No more skin cancer. In my many ears of using this method, I have never seen it fail to work!

Best of luck to you! And here are more specific instructions/advice.

Chapter Eight

Our "Super Dooper Skin Cancer Salve"

There are two ingredients in our Super Dooper salve.

Hydrogen Peroxide.

The main ingredient is liquid hydrogen peroxide. It is not just any-old drug store variety of peroxide. It is a special kind of hydrogen peroxide that is labeled **"35% Food Grade Hydrogen Peroxide"**.
This special peroxide can be found at many health food stores, or it can be bought online.

The last 16 oz. bottle that I bought cost me about $20.00. It will last me about 6 months.

35% Food Grade Hydrogen Peroxide

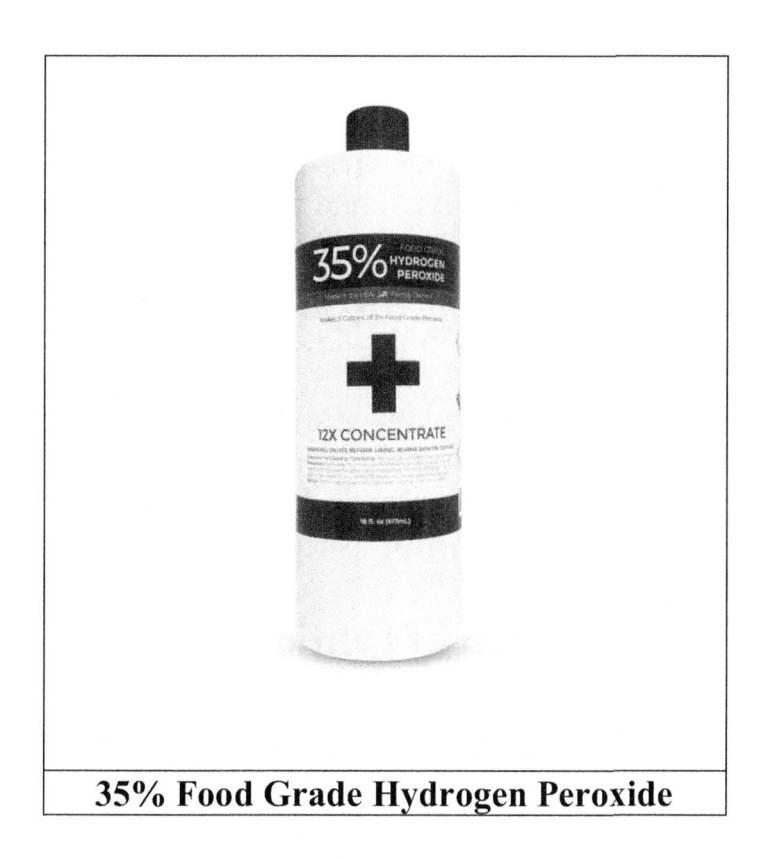

How it works.

The chemical expression for hydrogen peroxide is H_2O_2. When the hydrogen peroxide is placed on your skin, it transfers to H_2O (water) and O (a free molecule of oxygen). This free molecule of oxygen is very reactive. It wants to quickly bond with something else.

If the hydrogen peroxide has been placed on a malignant tumor (such as a skin cancer tumor) it will quickly bond with the tumor. But the cancerous tumor is anaerobic; it cannot exist in the presence of oxygen. Thus it immediately dies.

And that, dear friend is how it works. It works fast. It is simple to apply. And, in my many years of using this salve, I have never failed to see it work properly.

A few words of caution.

Hydrogen peroxide is very sensitive to light. If it is not stored in a dark place, it will deteriorate quickly. It should be kept is a light- proof bottle, and the bottle should be stored in a cool, dark place.

Also, it should be replaced every year-or-so. Age will reduce its strength.

Aloe Vera Gel.

Aloe Vera Gel

The other ingredient is aloe vera gel.

This is easier to obtain. You can find it at almost any drug store, grocery store, or health food store. A 16 oz. bottle or jar costs me about $16.00.

Making the Salve:

Making the salve is incredibly easy. Just mix up the amount that you will need. Make the ratio about 50% peroxide and 50% aloe vera gel. It is that simple.

You may want to use a plastic, wood or metal spoon for your mixing, as the 35% peroxide is very strong and may burn your fingers.

Store your salve in a light-proof bottle and keep in in a dark place (a refrigerator works fine).

Using the Salve:

Apply the salve to your skin cancer as needed. The more you apply, the faster it will act.

If, when you apply the salve, you see a bubbling action, this is a really good sign. The bubbling action is the active oxygen molecule in the peroxide mixing with the cancerous growth.

You should see results within a few days.

Chapter Nine

My Epiphany

Well, I have previously explained that arthritic pain had begun to cripple me. My aching knees were keeping me awake at night. My doctor suggested knee replacement surgery (ouch!). This forced me out of desperation to begin my own research. I had previously beaten cancer by discovering my own alternative remedy (Essiac Herbal Tea), so I was determined to do the same thing for my pain.

The Internet is a great research tool. Google led me to read about the acidity-arthritic connection. Amazon.com led me to great books about this subject. Authors such as Drs. Young, Baroody and Frassetto are pioneers in revealing the medical truths that have been touched lightly upon here in this booklet.

Then one morning, in my "quiet time" I strangely enough wandered back in my mind to a chemistry class that I had some 45 years ago. My chemistry professor had just written on the blackboard, "An acid plus a base makes a salt."

Could this be it? So simple! Our bodies have too much acid. If I ingest a base (baking soda, also known as sodium bicarbonate, jumped to mind) would it react with some of the acid in my body to make a salt, a salt that my body could easily expel? Wow. What an interesting idea. So I began daily eating about 8,000 mg (a small teaspoonful) of Arm and Hammer Baking Soda. I bought it at the grocery store. I mixed it with water. It tasted yucky. Within a month I began to see results. Within three months I began to regain my flexibility. All pain was gone. Later I had a chemist put the baking soda in capsules. That tasted much better. No more yucky taste.

So now, even though my arthritis has gone bye-bye, I still take my capsules daily. I test my pH weekly, keeping it always above 6.6 or 6.7. Usually it tests out at about 7.0. And I feel twenty years younger.

How Will You Know That It Is Working?

I previously mentioned that there are test strips that you can use to test your body's pH. Remember litmus paper in high school chemistry? It is very similar.

You can buy an inexpensive test kit.. I buy mine off the Internet. A test kit is shown on www.microessentiallab.com.

It is Catalog # 067, Hydrion Single Roll pH Paper and sells for $7.50.

I test my saliva in the morning before I have brushed my teeth or eaten anything.

How To Test For Your pH

Saliva pH is controlled by your diet and the amount of vitamins and minerals you have in your body. Lower saliva pH is a good indicator that the body is too acidic. Saliva pH over 7.0 is a good indicator that you are in excellent health.. This simple test is a good general way to measure the level of your acidity. The benefits of saliva pH testing are that it is simple, inexpensive, and the patient has control over monitoring their path back to good health. Saliva pH has been used by physicians for decades as a general indicator of your body's health, as well as the specific check we seek for treatment of diabetes or arthritis.

Recent research has linked low saliva pH to numerous leading diseases. Saliva pH is usually measured from 5-9, the lower your score the more acidic and the more likely you are to have health problems. Your ideal saliva pH level should be between 7.0-7.4, this is either 1st thing in the morning or an hour after any food or fluid intake. The good news is that you can monitor and improve your health without costly medications or doctors visits. You can improve your saliva pH by improving the foods you eat and the nutritional supplements you take. Then you can say goodbye to unhealthy symptoms.

Quotes From Knowledgeable Doctors:

The below information is extracted from the wonderful and informative books about

pH balance written by Dr. Robert O. Young, Microbiologist:

Forward in one book is by Chi C. Mao, M.D., Ph. D., Chief Medical Officer, Select Specialty Hospitals of Houston, Texas, a scientist who served previously at the National Institute of Health. He states:

1. According to mainstream medicine, arthritis and diabetes mellitus (either type 1 or type 2) have long been considered incurable.
2. Dr. Robert O. Young presents medical research, including clinical studies that suggest that a complete cure is possible.
3. Dr. Young's message is that "overacidification of our body fluids, due to our diet and modern lifestyles, is the origin of myriad pain and illnesses; therefore, in order to regain our health, it becomes imperative to minimize acidification and restore a critical balance."
4. Dr. Mao states, "It is my belief that Dr. Young's theory, his therapeutic methodology, and his commitment to

health care will continue to make history in years to come."

"[Disease] results, rather, from a disruption of the delicate pH balance (acid-base) in the fluids that surround the cells of the pancreas and other organs. Overacidity in the fluid allows cells to transform in negative ways, interfering with (among many other things) the way the body produces and uses its energy, and causing pain.

"[Disease] is the result of a pH imbalance in the fluids of the body –systemic acidosis- that interferes with the optimum functioning of the cells they surround. Beta cells surrounded by acids do not or cannot produce sufficient insulin. Acids destroy insulin receptor sites on the cellular membrane so body cells cannot properly use the hormone."

"The one indicator most crucial to your health [is] the pH of your blood"

"Acidity in different tissues of the body shows up with different sets of symptoms and pain, which have had various labels slapped on them by mainstream medical science. When the acidity is in the pancreas, diabetes is the result."

"In addition, when the blood is overly acid, it begins to unload the excess acids into the body's tissues, storing them in protective fat in the breasts, hips, belly, bone joints, and even in the brain, heart, and pancreas."

"It would seem that our fat is killing us. And far be it from me to argue for carrying around excess baggage. But the truth is, right now all that fat is probably *saving* your life. That's because the body uses fat to bind up and neutralize its excess acids, protecting all the tissues and organs that sustain life from acid damage."

How to ingest Baking Soda

Many people take baking soda to assist their health by mixing baking soda in water and drinking it. Baking soda mixed with water tastes yucky. So I have found a way to take my baking soda that is more pleasant.

1. Start off taking about a quarter of a teaspoon once or twice daily. Work up from this until you are taking ¾ to a full teaspoonful once or twice daily.
2. Place your dosage of baking soda in a large empty glass. Add an equal amount of Tang or sweetened Kool-Aid.
3. Fill the glass one-quarter full of water. Let whatever frothing occurs happen.
4. After the frothing has stopped, fill the glass the rest of the way with more water. Then stir thoroughly and drink.

I also mix some psyllium husk powder into my drink. Psyllium husks swell when they get to your stomach. This will give your stomach a full feeling, thus making dieting easier. And the psyllium husks also does a good job of cleaning your large intestine (colon). You can find bulk psyllium at many health food stores or order it off the Internet at sources such as herbalcom.com.

Additional Notes on taking Baking Soda:

The big problem with taking baking soda is the terrible taste. I have worked out a method for taking it that works for me and I would like to share it with you. Every day I make a jar of sun (solar) tea. Two or three times a day I do the following: I take an 8 oz. glass of the tea, add stevia to taste, and then add 1/3 heaping teaspoon of baking soda. I stir thoroughly, and enjoy the drink. It is actually enjoyable after a while. I sometimes add a small amount of orange juice or other juice to vary the taste. I am sure to add enough stevia to make the taste pleasant.

When an opened box of baking soda is kept in the pantry it absorbs bad odors. These odors accumulate in the baking soda, adding to its unpleasant taste. So when I open a fresh box of baking soda, I place it in a small glass jar so I can keep it sealed to keep bad tastes away from it. This makes a big difference in how the baking soda drink tastes.

Another helpful tip that will improve the taste of your baking soda: Only use plastic spoons or other utensils to handle your baking soda. The baking soda will actually pick up an unpleasant metallic taste from a metal spoon or scoop. So only use plastic. I was amazed at how the taste of my baking soda drink improved with this simple trick.

My goal is to keep my body ph above 6.2. I believe that cancer cannot exist in your body at this ph. It also will help the other afflictions stay away. I am enclosing several ebooks on this subject. I am indebted to Dr. R.O.Young and his research on the connection between body ph and disease.

Diabetes is a big problem these days. It is caused by over-acidity of the pancreas. So the baking soda will help but it may take time. Arthritis sufferers can see dramatic results within a month. Cancer people can see results within several months.

Big business has taken over aspects of our life. There is no money to be made with baking soda health therapies, so you will never hear much about it from the system. Sorry, but that is just the way it is.

Chapter Ten

Conclusion

I hope that I have shown you how to prevent disease, keep your skin and organs healthy, and how to alkalize your body so that the body's natural systems will dispose of your unhealthy conditions. It is so simple. Eat baking soda in an amount sufficient to remove the acidity from your body.

We read in our history books how the ancient Romans poisoned themselves by cooking in lead pots. Some historians even suggest that the resulting widespread lead poisoning of the general populace may have hastened the downfall of the Roman Empire.

We now know better than to eat in lead pots.

But could it just be that our own civilization is at a point where it is doing something equally stupid and disastrous? Could it be that many years from now students will read that our civilization weakened and perished because we over-acidified our bodies to the point that we poisoned ourselves and weakened our society? I have only to go to a shopping center and look at the shoppers. The general obesity and look of unhealthiness of our general populace is alarming.

I sincerely hope and pray that this small book will make a difference.

Attached is a copy of the informative and helpful book *Alternative Medicine Cancer Therapies.*

Addendum To Skin Cancer Health Book:

Edgar Cayce Information On Acidity

Some of this information is taken from the Meridian Institute Website .www.meridianinstitute.com

This background data is provided to assist you to understand the pain relief that is available for diabetes, arthritis, cancer and other diseases, pain relief, and their symptoms.

ACID/ALKALINE BALANCE

Edgar Cayce consistently emphasized the importance of maintaining a proper acid/alkaline balance in the body. Commonly referred to as "pH" (potential for hydrogen), the acid/alkaline continuum ranges from 0 - 14 with 7 as neutral. The lower end of the scale (below 7) is acid and above 7 is alkaline. Generally speaking, the Cayce readings maintain that a balanced pH with a slight alkaline tendency would be beneficial for most individuals.

Edgar Cayce noted that high systemic acidity either causes or contributes to many health problems. The items on Scale 5 are based on 133 readings which mention "superacidity" as an etiological factor. High systemic acidity (Scale 5) is often caused by eating a diet containing too much acid producing foods such as sweets and meats. Stress is another factor which can increase acidity. Improper food combinations (such as eating grains and citrus at the same meal) can result in high acidity.

Alkalinity can be increased by consuming less meat and sweets and more vegetables and fruits. Although eating fruit to increase alkalinity may seem to be a contradiction because some fruits (especially citrus) are acidic outside the body, digestion uses up their acidic components, leaving an alkaline residue (ash). Thus the net effect is alkaline-producing within the system. For most individuals, Cayce noted that "a normal diet is about twenty percent acid to eighty percent alkaline-producing." Appendix F contains an acid/alkaline table that lists the Ph of common foods.

According to Cayce, numerous factors can increase acidity (and pain) including negative emotional states, inadequate mastication of food, and poor eliminations. Perhaps the most common factor cited by Cayce is diet. Eating acid-producing foods or combining foods improperly (even akaline-producing foods) is said to lead to hyperacidity, even to "superacidity" in some instances.

Cayce sometimes observed that infectious agents (such as virus and bacteria) do not thrive in an alkaline environment: "cold CANNOT - DOES NOT - exist in alkalines." Thus, consuming alkaline-producing foods (such as orange juice and lemon juice) was recommended to prevent colds.

The antimicrobial influence of alkalinity is supported by research on goldenseal, a well-known antibacterial herb. Berberine sulfate, the most active antibacterial alkaloid in goldenseal, is more effective in an alkaline than an acid environment. At a pH of 8.0 (alkaline), its antimicrobial activity in vitro is about 2 to 4 times greater than at 7.0 (neutral). At an acid pH of 6.0, the antimicrobial activity is only 1/4 as strong as at a neutral pH.

Acid/alkaline balance is extremely important to normal physiology. For example, the blood will maintain a slightly alkaline range of 7.35 to 7.45. Extended pH imbalances of any kind are not well tolerated by the body. The management of the pH factor is so important that the body has developed strict accounting procedures to monitor acid-alkaline balances in every cell and system. The fundamental regulatory systems of the body (including breathing, circulation, elimination, etc.) affect pH balance.

Edgar Cayce insisted that acid/alkaline balance could be easily checked. Numerous readings encourage the measurement of pH balance in saliva and urine as an objective means of monitoring this crucial aspect of physiology.

Author's note: Edgar Cayce, in some of his readings actually recommended consuming baking soda as a remedy for overacidity. So he beat me to my discovery. But I don't mind!

Chapter Eleven

Alternative Cancer Therapies That Have Worked For Thousands

Seven Natural Cancer Remedies

That Are Effective, Inexpensive,

And Readily Available

Alternative Medicine Cancer Therapies That Have Worked For Thousands

Copyright 2001

Freedom12 Press

Table of Contents

Introduction: Why You Should Read This Book

Chapter 1. Oxygen Therapy

Chapter 2. Essiac Tea: the Indian Herbal Remedy

Chapter 3. Kombucha the Amazing Mushroom Tea

Chapter 4. Pycnogenol and Grape Seed Extract

Chapter 5. Colon Health and Cancer

Chapter 6. Cancer and the Parasite Connection

Chapter 7. MGN-3

Chapter 8. Summary and Conclusion

Why You Should Read This Book

The typical practicing physician gets office visits from two categories of people. He gets visited by his patients, and typically he has a waiting room full of patients. He also gets visited, and frequently, by pharmaceutical reps. The pharmaceutical reps are there for several purposes. First, they are there as a reminder for the physician to keep using their company's drug products. But they are there also to brief the physician on their company's latest product developments. They will present the latest technical reports, and sales literature, and free samples, to the doctor. In this way each doctor keeps abreast of the latest developments in his field.

We all know how busy doctors are. The drug company's pharmaceutical reps perform a valuable service to the doctor, and the patients, by keeping the doctor fully informed and educated on the latest developments in the drug industry. The doctor does not have to go home at night and take part of his valuable and scarce private time to study about pharmaceutical advances; he is taught right in his office.

So when you come in to your doctor's office to report that you have cancer, the doctor is already up-to-date on the latest techniques advocated by the pharmaceutical companies for treating cancer. Is it any wonder then that this harried and overworked professional will prescribe a therapy to treat your cancer that follows the recommendations of the pharmaceutical companies? In addition, in medical school he was only taught cancer therapies that were approved by the American Medical Association that is heavily influenced and controlled by the pharmaceutical drug companies. Then, with his busy schedule, he just does not have the time or inclination to search out any natural and inexpensive cancer treatments that might serve you well.

This, of course, does not apply to all doctors. As awareness of the benefits of certain natural alternative cancer therapies become better known among the general populace, many brave doctors are venturing afield into holistic and natural medicines. But to do so places them at risk of censure and ridicule by their peers, as well as formal censure or loss of license to practice medicine.

The point I am making here is that your doctor, for one reason or another, may not tell you all that you need to know about the therapies which would best cure your cancer. So it may be up to you to seek out other sources of information, such as this book.

Those of you who may wish further information about the travails and misfortunes which may befall any doctor who "swims against the current" of conventional medical wisdom should search the Internet for the facts about Dr. Stanislaw Burzynski of Texas, who discovered a cure for certain types of cancer. He has been kept out of prison only because of the widespread support of many other brave physicians who have gone to bat for him. But his career and finances have been ruined because of persecution by the medical establishment. You may find an article about his situation on the Internet at .www.alkalizeforhealth.net/Lburzynski.htm.

There is a historical precedent for this type of situation. It took the medical establishment over fifty years to accept antibiotics! Yes, it is true. Penicillin, the first antibiotic, was discovered in the early 1890s. But the medical profession scoffed at the claims made about penicillin, and its use was ridiculed and scorned. It was not until World War II in the 1940s, when the medical profession was overwhelmed with the wounded and injured of war, that penicillin was tried on a mass scale and given a chance to prove its worth. The problem here is that you and I do not wish to wait fifty years for the medical establishment to approve natural effective remedies for cancer. We do not have the time.

Chapter 1. Oxygen Therapy

The cancer virus is anaerobic. This means that it can only live in the absence of oxygen. As a matter of fact, exposure to oxygen will kill this virus. The HIV virus is anaerobic. Exposure to oxygen will kill it. As a matter of fact, most disease causing viruses are anaerobic. They can only live where there is a low level of oxygen.

This fact becomes most interesting when it is noted that anaerobic viruses can only live in our body when the oxygen carrying capacity of our blood decreases to 60% of its optimum level. This has been known for some time. In 1931 Dr. Otto Warburg was awarded the Nobel Prize for Medicine for his discovery that he had found the cause of cancer to be a lack of oxygen at the cellular level. In 1953 the National Cancer Institute endorsed Dr. Warburg's findings. Additional observations:

Dr. Albert Wahl: "Disease is due to a deficiency in the oxidation process of the body, leading to an accumulation of toxins. These toxins are ordinarily burned in normal oxidation."

Dr. Harry Goldblatt (<u>Journal of Experimental Medicine</u>): "Lack of oxygen clearly plays a major role in causing cells to become cancerous."

Dr. Steven Levine: "Hypoxia, or the lack of oxygen in the tissues, is the fundamental cause of all degenerative diseases."

Dr. John Muntz: "Starved of oxygen the body will become ill, and if this persists it will die. I doubt that there is any argument about that."

There is clearly a correlation between the levels of oxygen in our body and illness. It is important to note that <u>fear, anxiety, worry,</u>

and depression all interfere with the breathing process, and will reduce the oxygen intake. This can lead to illness. But there is an even greater problem facing our bodies and their needs for an adequate supply of oxygen. It concerns the very air we breathe.

The Oxygen Story

Remember the movie Jurassic Park? In this movie, Scientists extracted DNA from the blood of mosquitoes, which were imbedded in fossilized amber in order to recreate prehistoric animals. Well, something similar has happened in real life. In the laboratory, real life scientists have extracted air, which was trapped as bubbles in fossilized amber. When the air was analyzed, it was found to contain 38% oxygen. This is very noteworthy because the air we breathe today has an average oxygen content of 21% or less.

The significance of this is immense. As man has evolved from his primitive prehistoric form, the oxygen levels of the air he breathes have dropped 50%. The implications of this on our health may be staggering. What if the human body was designed to live and prosper on air that contained 38% oxygen, a level that is 50% higher than the air we breathe today? What if the reduced levels of oxygen in the air we breathe today are causing our bodies to not receive an adequate level of oxygen for them to be well and healthy?

In fact, the air in various areas of the world is declining in oxygen content. In other words, this situation is getting worse. In some of the larger, more pollution plagued cities, the oxygen levels of air have declined as low as 15%. Man cannot live at levels at 7% oxygen or lower, even for a short period of time. It is safe to say that mankind may be facing a serious problem here.

Other Problems

We do not plan to go into great detail here about the other conditions in our lives, which result in our blood not carrying an adequate supply of oxygen to the muscles and cells of our bodies. In general, we have depleted our soils by the overuse of chemical fertilizers, resulting in our foodstocks not providing us with adequate nutrition. Example: Vegetables today have only 25% of the minerals and enzymes of vegetables grown 90 years ago. And many of the fruits and vegetables come to us contaminated with insecticides and pesticides. The consumption of processed salt, which has 82 of its 84 minerals and trace elements removed, and is coated with aluminum hydroxide which makes it insoluble in our bodies, harms our health. Most of the meat we consume today contains growth hormones and antibiotics, giving new meaning to the expression "you are what you eat." All of these factors lead to a lower level of overall health and energy, and a condition where our weakened bodies become overloaded with toxins. It is the job of our blood to extract these toxins from the cells of our bodies, and carry the toxins to the wall of the large intestine (colon). There the toxins are passed through the wall of the intestine, to be carried away with the waste products of our body.

But there is a problem here. The long-term consumption of too many processed foods has resulted in our large intestines becoming sluggish, which has led to a buildup on the intestinal walls of a hardened mucous-like coating. The average 50 year-old-American Male has a coating lining his colon, which weighs 5 pounds! It acts like a barrier between the wall of the large intestine (colon) and the waste products passing through the colon. As a result, the blood is not able to easily pass the toxins it is carrying through the wall of the colon. Unable to unload its toxins, the blood is forced to continue carrying the toxins. Under better conditions, the blood, after unloading its load of toxins, would pick up a load of oxygen to carry to the cells on its return trip. But now, still loaded with toxins, the blood is unable to carry oxygen back to the body's cells. Oxygen starvation results.

The Symptoms of Oxygen Deficiency

Doctors and scientists have identified the initial symptoms of oxygen deprivation, which actually constitutes the gradual oxygen starvation of the body's seven trillion cells. In addition to illness, these symptoms are:

- overall body weakness
- muscle aches
- depression

- fatigue
- arthritis

- irrational behavior

- irritability & dizziness
- memory loss
- hostility

- circulation problems
- poor digestion
- lowered immunity to colds, flu, infection
- bronchial problems
- tumors and deposit buildups
- bacterial, viral and parasitic infestations
- circulation problems
- acid stomach

People rarely suspect that the above conditions, or the constant vague feelings of helplessness, fatigue or despair is the result of the cells of their body desperately sending out signals that they need more oxygen.

The Use of Oxygen Therapies

By now I hope that I have convinced you of the need to get more oxygen to the cells of your body. You have probably surmised that if we could add oxygen directly to

> **Ozone machines have become portable and affordable**

the blood in your body, most of the disturbing problems discussed above could be overcome. You are right. There are a number of ways to accomplish this. One approach is ozone therapy. Regular oxygen is O2. Ozone is O3, that is, each molecule has an extra atom of oxygen. When ozone is added to your body, the extra oxygen atom immediately leaves the ozone, and attached itself to a cell of your body. Your oxygen level is thereby increased. Chemically, the ozone (O3) has become oxygen (O2) plus oxygen (O). Ozone Therapy is widely practiced in other countries. In Germany, equipment and procedures have become refined to the point that doctors there can remove sluggish, toxin loaded blood from your body, ozonate the blood, remove the toxins, and reinsert the now oxygen enriched blood back into the patient's body. Other less complicated procedures involve using a relatively simple ozone machine to add ozone to the body through rectal insufflations, use of body wraps, or by simply drinking ozonated water. Wondrous cures for a wide litany of illnesses have been effected with ozone therapy. However, ozone therapy is not practiced in the United States.

Another procedure is the use of food grade hydrogen peroxide (H2O2). When hydrogen peroxide is added to the body, the H2O2 quickly becomes H2O (water) plus O (oxygen atom). The oxygen atom attaches itself to a cell of your body, and again, your oxygen level has just gone up. It is <u>very important</u> here to note that the type of hydrogen peroxide (3%), which is typically sold in drug stores and grocery stores, <u>cannot be used</u> for such a purpose. It contains contaminants and is dangerous for such use. Food Grade Hydrogen Peroxide (35%) is available through many health food stores. Food Grade Hydrogen Peroxide is the only type of hydrogen peroxide that can be used. Diluted Food Grade Hydrogen Peroxide can be given intravenously, or absorbed through the skin, or injested. One method which has successfully been used by many is to add 4 to 6 ounces of Food Grade 35% hydrogen peroxide to a tub of hot water and soak for 45 to 60 minutes. This is done daily. The hydrogen peroxide passes thru the skin into the blood stream where it is converted into oxygen. Miraculous recoveries from cancer, arthritis, Epstein Barr, chronic fatigue, lupus, multiple sclerosis, diabetes, allergies, and many other illnesses have been reported.

Why Doesn't Your Doctor Tell You This?

All oxygen therapies, including hydrogen peroxide therapy, are non-patentable processes. They are for the most part also inexpensive, and in many cases can be administered at home by the patient. Therefore there is no financial incentive for the pharmaceutical industry or the American Medical Association to promote these therapies. As a matter of fact, they will discipline severely any doctor caught using oxygen therapy.

This is not the case in certain other countries. In Germany, Russia, and Cuba, for example, physicians have successfully treated many serious and chronic conditions.

Cancer, heart disease, AIDS, chronic fatigue, and many other illnesses have been successfully treated. In these countries a treatment consisting of a medical infusion of hydrogen peroxide costs approximately $10. No financial incentive here for the pharmaceutical industry, medical centers, and physicians who are accustomed to providing expensive drugs, and complex medical procedures. Thus, knowledge of this esoteric field is restricted to those intellectually courageous individuals who venture into the realms of alternative medicine.

What Can Be Done?

We have reviewed all of the oxygen therapy methods available, analyzed the cost and practicality of their application, and have reached a conclusion. Drinking water that contains a minute amount of food grade hydrogen peroxide is a good procedure. Many people have significantly increased the oxygen content of their blood, thereby improving their health or overcoming their illness, by this simple protocol. First of all, as we emphasize, use only 35% Food Grade Hydrogen Peroxide. Keep it in the refrigerator, or in a cool dark place (light will damage it). Use only distilled water, or reverse osmosis filtered water. This is because the iron content of regular water will react with the hydrogen peroxide to impart an unpleasant taste to the water. Carefully place 10 drops of the 35% hydrogen peroxide in an 8 oz. glass of distilled water, and immediately drink. Drink 5 glasses of this peroxide water daily. Best if taken on an empty stomach (it will taste better). That's it. Simple and cheap. And effective. Also, soaking daily in a tub of water to which 4 to 6 oz. of food grade hydrogen peroxide has been added, as already mentioned above, is a good therapy.

Mail Order Sources of Food Grade 35% Hydrogen Peroxide

First check with Google for an Internet source. Then check your local health food store. It may stock 35% food grade hydrogen peroxide. If not, you may obtain it from:

1. Sullivan Creek Distributing Co., 955 73rd Ave. NE. Carrington ND 58421, Toll Free Telephone: 888-406-4066, sells a 16 oz. bottle of food grade 35% hydrogen peroxide for $16.95.
2. Raw Health Inc., 11355 SW 14th St, Beaverton OR 97005, Telephone 866-729-4584, sells a 32 oz. bottle of food grade 35% hydrogen peroxide for $18.00.
3. Pure Health Systems, Telephone 970-731-9724 sells 35% food grade hydrogen peroxide. A 16 oz. bottle is $16.95 and a gallon bottle is $55.00.

Note: We are researchers, not physicians. Consult your physician. This researched information does not make any claims. It is not intended to replace sound medical advice.

Additional Reading

For additional reading, Crossroads, Toll Free Tel: 800-635-5823 sells books about oxygen therapy. I recommend *Oxygen Therapies* by Ed McCabe, and *Hydrogen*

Peroxide and Ozone by Conrad LeBeau (only $3.95).

Bibliography

Oxygen by Dr. Kurt Donsbach, The Rockland Corporation, Tel: 800 421 7310

Bio/Tech News, newsletter, PO Box 30568, Parkrose Center, Portland OR 97294

The Story of Ozone, Plasmafire Intl., 7186-205 St. Langley, B.C., V2Y1T1 Canada

Oxygen Therapies by Ed McCabe, $14.00 from Books, 4100 Bonita Rd. Santa Monica CA 91902

Alternatives newsletter by Dr. David G.Williams, PO Box 829, Ingram TX 78025

Health & Healing newsletter by Dr. Julian Whittaker, Phillips Publishing, 7811 Montrose Rd., Potomac MD 20854

Chapter 2. Essiac Tea: the Ojibwa Herbal Remedy from Canada

Essiac tea has a proven track record of curing thousands of cancer. Among its many reported properties, it attacks directly cancer tumors, detoxifies the body, removes heavy metals, and it builds up the immune system. It has also been found effective as a treatment for AIDS, lupus, chronic fatigue syndrome, diabetes, and many other illnesses. That such a simple remedy exists, is so widely unknown, and continues to be ignored by the mainstream medical establishment, is an amazing story.

The Essiac Story:

Rene Caisse was a nurse in Canada. In 1923 she observed that one of her doctor's patients, a woman with terminal cancer, made a complete recovery. Inquiring into the matter, Rene found that the woman had used an herbal remedy given to her by an Ojibway Indian herbalist. Rene visited the Indian medicine man, and he gladly and freely presented her with his tribe's formula. He explained to her that the Ojibway used their tonic both for spiritual balance and body healing. The formula consisted of four common herbs. They were blended and cooked in a fashion that caused the concoction to have a greater curative power than any of the four herbs themselves. The four herbs were Sheep Sorrel, Burdock Root, Slippery Elm Bark, and Rhubarb Root.

With her doctor's permission, Rene began to administer the herbal remedy to other terminal cancer patients who had been given up by the medical profession as incurable. Most recovered.

Rene then began to collect the herbs herself, prepare the remedy in her own kitchen, and to treat hundreds of cancer cases. She set up a clinic in Bracebridge, Ontario where she administered the herbal remedy free to all who sought her help. She found that Essiac, as she named the herbal remedy, could not undo the effects of severe damage to the life support organs. In such cases, however, the pain of the illness was alleviated and the life of the patients was extended longer than predicted. In the other cases, where the life support organs had not been severely damaged, cure was complete, and the patients lived another 35 or 40 years. Some are still alive today.

Rene selflessly dedicated herself to helping these patients. She continued to treat hundreds of patients from her home. She did not charge for her services. Donations were her only income. They barely kept her above the poverty line. Over the years word of her work began to spread. The Canadian medical establishment did not take kindly to this nurse administering this remedy directly to anyone with cancer who requested her help. Thus began many years of harassment and persecution by the Canadian Ministry of Health and Welfare. Word of this struggle was carried throughout Canada by newspapers.

The newspaper coverage of Rene's work began to make her famous. Word was also spread far and wide by the families of those healed by Essiac. Eventually, the Royal Cancer Commission became interested in her work. They undertook to study Essiac.

In 1937 the Royal Cancer Commission conducted hearings about Essiac. Eventually the Canadian Parliament, prodded by the newspaper coverage and the widespread support generated for Rene by former patients and grateful families, voted in 1938 on legislation to legalize the use of Essiac. Fifty-five thousand signatures were collected on a petition presented to the Parliament. The vote was close, but Essiac failed by three votes to be approved as an officially sanctioned cure for cancer.

Rene continued her work for 60 years. In the 1960s, Rene Caisse worked with the well-known Brusch Clinic in Massachusetts. Dr. Charles A. Brusch was the personal physician for President John F. Kennedy. After 10 years of research about Essiac, Dr. Brusch made the following statement: "Essiac is a cure for cancer, period. All studies done at laboratories in the United

States and Canada support this conclusion". Rene Caisse died in 1978.

There are several excellent books about Essiac Tea. I recommend "Essiac: A Native Herbal Cancer Remedy" by Cynthia Olsen ($12.50) and "Essiac Essentials: The Remarkable Herbal Cancer Fighter" by Sheila Snow ($9.60). These books may be ordered online at .www.amazon.com or ordered from your local bookstore.

What It Is

Rene Caisse's herbal formula contains four commonly occurring herbs:

Sheep Sorrel (Rumex acetosella).

The leaves of young Sheep Sorrel plants were popular as a cooking dressing and as an addition to salads in France several hundred years ago. Indians also use Sheep Sorrel leaves as a tasty seasoning for meat dishes. They also baked it into their bread. Thus it is both an herb and a food.

Sheep Sorrel belongs to the buckwheat family. Common names for Sheep Sorrel are field sorrel, red top sorrel, sour grass and dog eared sorrel. It should not be confused with Garden Sorrel. (Rumex acetosa).

Sheep Sorrel grows wild throughout most of the world. It seeks open pastures, rocky areas, and the shoulders of country roads. It is considered to be a common weed throughout the U. S. The entire Sheep Sorrel plant may be harvested to be used in Essiac. Or, just the leaves and stems may be harvested, and this allows the plants to be "reharvested" later. The plant portion of the Sheep Sorrel may be harvested throughout the spring, summer, and fall. Harvest the leaves and stem before the flowers begin to form, since at this stage, all of the energy of the plant is in the leaves.

Burdock Root (Arctium lappa).

The roots, young stems, and seeds of the Burdock plant are edible. Young stalks are boiled to be eaten like asparagus. Raw stems and young leaves are eaten in salads. Parts of the Burdock plant are eaten in China, Hawaii, and among the Native American cultures on this continent. It is then, both an herb and a food.

The Burdock is a member of the thistle family. Remember the last time you cleaned cockleburs from your clothing after a sojourn in the woods or meadow? Chances are, you had run up against this very friendly and helpful plant, you just didn't know it! It is a common pasture weed throughout North America. It prefers damp soils. The first years the Burdock plant produces only green leafy growth. It is during the second year that it produces the long sturdy stems with annoying burrs.

The root of the Burdock plant is harvested. It is harvested from only the first year plants. The roots are about an inch wide, and up to three feet long. As with the Sheep Sorrel, the roots
should only be harvested in the Fall when the plant energy is concentrated in the roots.

Slippery Elm (Ulcus fulva).

The inner bark of the Slippery Elm tree has a long history of use as a food supplement and herbal remedy. Pioneers knew of it as a survival food. The powdered bark has long been used, and is still being used today, as a food additive and food extender, rich in vitamin and mineral content. Thus it also is both an herb and a food. The Slippery Elm is a favorite shade and ornamental tree. It is found throughout Canada and the United States. Only the inner bark of the Slippery Elm is used to make Essiac.

Turkey Rhubarb (Rheum palmatum).

We have all eaten Rhubarb. Its red, bittersweet stems are to be found in supermarket produce shelves each spring. We also eat rhubarb pie, jams and pudding. The Turkey Rhubarb is a member of the rhubarb family with roots that contain a particularly strong and desirable potency.

The Turkey Rhubarb grows in China. The roots are harvested when the plants are at least six years old. This imported product has more potency than our native rhubarb. Rene Caisse began her Essiac work using the domestic rhubarb root, later discovering that the imported variety was more potent and less bitter. However most of the Turkey Rhubarb that is now imported into this country is irradiated, so that native rhubarb is now once again the rhubarb of choice.

The Formula

The original formula, as given by Rene Caisse, is listed below: Please note that she made large batches for many patients, and we are reprinting here her exact instructions for a two gallon batch, although you would probably not need such a large amount at one time.

Ingredients:
52 parts: Burdock Root (cut or dried) (parts by weight).
16 parts: Sheep Sorrel (powdered)
1 part: Turkey Rhubarb Root (powdered) or 2 parts native Rhubarb Root
4 parts: Slippery Elm Bark (powdered)

This is the basic four-herb formula that was presented to the Royal Cancer Commission in 1937 and was found by them to be a "cure for cancer". Later in her life, while working with Dr. Charles Brusch in Massachusetts, Rene added small potentizing amounts of four other herbs to her basic four-herb formula. They were added as follows: Kelp (2 parts), Red Clover (1 part), Blessed Thistle (1 part), Watercress (0.4 parts). I consider the addition of these four extra herbs optional.

Preparation: The above ingredients are boiled for ten minutes in two gallons of water. Then the mixture is allowed to cool and set for approximately 12 hours. Then it is reheated to boiling and strained and bottled.

Instructions for Use

1. Keep refrigerated.
2. Shake bottle well before using.
3. May be taken either cold from the bottle, or warmed (never microwave).
4. As a Preventative, daily take 4 tablespoons (2 ounces) at bedtime or on an empty stomach at least 2 hours after eating.
5. People with cancer and other people with

health challenges may wish to twice daily take 4 tablespoons (2 ounces), once in the morning, 5 minutes before eating, and once in the evening, at least 2 hours after eating.

Note:

a. Stomach Cancer patients must dilute the herbal drink with an equal amount of sodium free distilled water.
b. Many people have reported that Rene's drink works well to detoxify the body, and have taken it as a detoxification program.
c. Precaution: Some doctors advise against taking the herbal formula while pregnant.

Recommendation: Rene reported that the twelve-hour brewing process is essential for Essiac to have its special powers. Essiac is now being offered to the public in pills, teabags, and homeopathic drops. We do not recommend them. They may work, but they are not what Rene used, nor have we seen evidence that they work.

What It Does

The components of Rene's herbal drink interact to have an amazing effect on the human body. The chemicals, minerals, and vitamins all act synergistically together to produce a variety of healing agents.

Sheep Sorrel:

Sorrel plants have been a folk remedy for cancer for centuries both in Europe and America. Sheep Sorrel has been observed by researchers to break down tumors, and to alleviate some chronic conditions and degenerative diseases.

It contains high amounts of vitamins A and B complex, C,D,E,K,P and vitamin U. It is also rich in minerals, including calcium, chlorine, iron, magnesium, silicon, sodium, sulphur, and has trace amounts of copper, iodine, manganese and zinc. The combination of these vitamins and minerals nourishes all of the glands of the body. Sheep Sorrel also contains carotenoids and chlorophyll, citric, malic, oxalic, tannic and tartaric acids.

The chlorophyll carries oxygen throughout the bloodstream. Cancer cells do not live in the presence of oxygen. It also:

- reduces the damage of radiation burns
- increases resistance to X-rays
- improves the vascular system, heart function, intestines, and lungs
- destroys parasites in the body
- aids in the removal of foreign deposits from the walls of the blood vessels
- purifies the liver, stimulates the growth of new tissue
- reduces inflammation of the pancreas, stimulates the growth of new tissue
- raises the oxygen level of the tissue cells

Sheep Sorrel is the primary healing herb in Essiac.

Burdock Root

For centuries Burdock has been used throughout the world to cure illness and disease. The root of the Burdock is a powerful blood purifier. It clears congestion in respiratory, lymphatic, urinary and circulatory systems. It promotes the flow of bile, and eliminates excess fluid in the body. It stimulates the elimination of toxic wastes, relieves liver malfunctions, and improves digestion. The Chinese use Burdock Root as an aphrodisiac, tonic, and rejuvenator. It assists in removing infection from the urinary tract, the liver, and the gall bladder. It expels toxins through the skin and urine. It destroys parasites. It is good against arthritis, rheumatism, and sciatica.

Burdock Root contains vitamins A, B complex, C, E, and P. It contains high amounts of chromium, cobalt, iron, magnesium, phosphorus, potassium, silicon, and zinc. It also contains smaller amounts of calcium, copper, manganese, selenium, and sulphur.

Much of the Burdock Root's curative power is attributed to its principal ingredient of Unulin, which helps to strengthen vital organs, especially the liver, pancreas, and spleen.

Slippery Elm Inner Bark

Slippery Elm Bark is widely known throughout the world as an herbal remedy. As a tonic it is known for its ability to sooth and strengthen the organs, tissues, and mucous membranes, especially the lungs and stomach. It promotes fast healing of cuts, burns, ulcers and wounds. It revitalizes the entire body.

It contains, as its primary ingredient, a mucilage, as well as quantities of gallic acid, phenols, starches, sugars, the vitamins A, B complex, C, K, and P. It contains large amounts of calcium, magnesium, and sodium, as well as lesser amounts of chromium and selenium, and trace amounts of iron, phosphorous, silicon and zinc.

Slippery Elm Bark is known among herbalists for its ability to cleanse, heal, and strengthen the body.

Rhubarb Root

Rhubarb, also a well-known herb, has been used worldwide since 220 BC as a medicine.

The Rhubarb root exerts a gentle laxative action by stimulating the secretion of bile into
the intestines. It also stimulates the gall duct

to expel toxic waste matter, thus purging the body of waste bile and food. As a result, the liver is cleansed, and chronic liver problems are relieved.

Rhubarb root contains vitamin A, many of the B complex, C, and P. Its high mineral content includes calcium, chlorine, copper, iodine, iron, magnesium, manganese, phosphorous, potassium, silicon, sodium, sulphur, and zinc.

Reported Benefits of Essiac:

1. Prevents the buildup of excess fatty deposits in artery walls, heart, kidney and liver.
2. Regulates cholesterol levels by transforming sugar and fat into energy.
3. Destroys parasites in the digestive system and throughout the body.
4. Counteracts the detrimental effects of aluminum, lead and mercury poisoning.
5. Strengthens and tightens muscles, organs and tissues.
6. Makes bones, joints, ligaments, lungs, and

membranes strong and flexible, less vulnerable to stress or stress injuries.
7. Nourishes and stimulates the brain and nervous system.
8. Promotes the absorption of fluids in the tissues.
9. Removes toxic accumulations in the fat, lymph, bone marrow, bladder, and alimentary canals.
10. Neutralizes acids, absorbs toxins in the bowel, and eliminates both.
11. Clears the respiratory channels by dissolving and expelling mucus.
12. Relieves the liver of its burden of detoxification by converting fatty toxins into water-soluble substances that can then be easily eliminated through the kidneys.
13. Assists the liver to produce lecithin, which forms part of the myelin sheath, a white fatty material that encloses nerve fibers.
14. Reduces, perhaps eliminates, heavy metal deposits in tissues (especially those surrounding the joints) to reduce inflammation and stiffness.
15. Improves the functions of the pancreas and spleen by increasing the effectiveness of insulin.
16. Purifies the blood.

17. Increases red cell production, and keeps them from rupturing.
18. Increases the body's ability to utilize oxygen by raising the oxygen level in the tissue cells.
19. Maintains the balance between potassium and sodium within the body so that the fluid inside and outside each cell is regulated: in this way, cells are nourished with nutrients and are also cleansed.
20. Converts calcium and potassium oxalates into a harmless form by making them solvent in the urine. It also regulates the amount of oxalic acid delivered to the kidneys, thus reducing the risk of stone formation in the gall bladder, kidneys, or urinary tract.
21. Protects against toxins entering the brain.
22. Protects the body against radiation and X-rays.
23. Relieves pain, increases appetite, and provides more energy along with giving a sense of well-being.
24. Speeds up wound healing by regenerating the damaged area.
25. Increases the production of antibodies like lymphocytes and T-cells in the thymus gland, which is the defender of our immune

system.
26. Inhibits and possibly destroys benign growths and tumors.
27. Protects the cells against free radicals.

An Endorsement by Dr. Julian Whitaker, M.D.

Dr. Julian Whitaker publishes a very informative and enlightening monthly newsletter named *Health and Healing*. It has 430,000 subscribers. In his November 1995 issue, he had an article entitled "What I Would Do If I Had Cancer". He states that if he had cancer he personally would follow a regime that included Essiac Tea.

Dr. Whitaker has over twenty years' experience. He has written five major health books: *Reversing Heart Disease, Reversing Diabetes, Reversing Health Risks, A Guide to Natural Healing* and *Is Heart Surgery Necessary?* Dr. Whitaker directs the Whitaker Wellness Institute in Newport Beach, California, which has treated thousands of patients. Should you desire information about subscribing to his newsletter, call (800) 705-5559.

I highly recommend this newsletter to anyone who has a serious illness and wishes to become more knowledgeable about the complete range of healing modalities available. He also proscribes a 7-step, 30-day wellness program "that will turn your life around."

Quotes from Rene Caisse:

"Though I worked each day from 9am to 9pm, my work was so absorbing there was no sense of fatigue. My waiting room was a place of happiness where people exchanged their experiences and shared their hope. After a few treatments, patients seemed to throw off their depression, fear and distress. Their outlook became optimistic and as their pain decreased, they became happy and talkative."

"I could see the changes in some of the patients. A number of them, presented to me by their doctors after everything known to medical science had been tried and failed, were literally carried into my clinic for their first treatment. To later see these same people walk in on their own, after only five or six treatments, more than repaid me for all my endeavours. I have helped thousands of such people. I offered the treatment at no charge."

"Most importantly, and this was verified in animal tests conducted at the Brusch Medical Centre and other laboratories, it was discovered that one of the most dramatic effects of taking this remedy was its affinity for drawing all of the cancer cells which had spread, back to the original site at which point the tumour would first harden, then later soften until it vanished altogether. In other cases, the tumour would decrease in size to where it could be surgically removed with minimal complications."

Source List of Suppliers

I recommend Natural Heritage Enterprises, PO Box 278, Crestone CO 81131, Toll Free Telephone: 888-568-3036. http://www.remedies.net. They sell Essiac

Tea in bottles and also in a less expensive package of dried herbs for those who wish to brew their own tea. I like their bonus buy: purchase 12 and get 6 additional for free (18 bottles of tea or 18 packages of herbs for the price of 12).

Bottles: Bottles of the herbal remedy can be purchased by mail order for $14.50 per 16 oz. bottle (a 4 day supply).

Dried Herbal Mix: Should you wish to prepare your own Essiac herbal drink, you may mail order packets of the dried herb combination. Each packet will allow you to prepare approximately one half gallon of the drink (a two week supply). The cost is $12.00 per packet.

Essiac Testimonials

```
         CHARLES A BRUSCH, M.D.
            15 GROZIER ROAD
          CAMBRIDGE, MA 02138
```

TO WHOM IT MAY CONCERN:

Many years have gone by since I first experienced the use of ESSIAC with my patients who were suffering from many varied forms of cancer.

I personally monitored the use of this old therapy along with Rene Caisse R.N., whose many successes were widely reported. Rene worked with me at my medical clinic in Cambridge, Massachusetts where, under the supervision of 18 of my medical doctors on staff, she proceeded with a series of treatments on terminal cancer patients and laboratory mice. Together we refined and perfected her formula.

On mice it has been shown to cause a decided recession of the mass and a definite change in cell formation. Clinically, on patients suffering from pathologically proven cancer, it reduces pain and causes a recession in growth. Patients gained weight and showed a great improvement in their general health. Their elimination improved considerably and their appetite became whetted.

Remarkably beneficial results were obtained even on those cases at the "end of the road", where it proved to prolong life and the "quality" of that life. In some cases, if the tumour didn't disappear, it could be surgically removed after ESSIAC with less risk of metastases resulting in new outbreaks.

Hemorrhage has been rapidly brought under control in many difficult cases, open lesions of lip and breast respond to treatment, and patients with cancer of the stomach have returned to normal activity among many other remembered cases. Also, intestinal burns from radiation were healed and damage replaced, and it was found to greatly improve whatever the condition.

All the patient cases were diagnosed by reputable physicians and surgeons. I do know that I have witnessed in my clinic, and know of many other cases, where ESSIAC was the therapy used - a treatment which brings about restoration through destroying the tumour tissue and improving the mental outlook which re-establishes physiological function.

I endorse this therapy even today for I have in fact cured my own cancer, the original site of which was the lower bowel, through ESSIAC alone. My last complete examination, when I was examined throughout the intestinal tract while hospitalized (August, 1989) for a hernia problem, revealed no sign of malignancy. Medical documents validate this. I have taken ESSIAC every day since my diagnosis (1984) and my recent examination has given me a clear bill of health.

I remained a partner with Rene Caisse until her death in 1978 and was the only person who had her complete trust and to whom she confided her knowledge and "know-how" of what she named "ESSIAC."

Others have imitated, but a minor success rate should never be accepted when the true therapy is available.

Executed as a legal document.

Signed: Charles A. Brusch, M.D., April 11, 1990

Editor's Note: Dr. Brusch was JFK's personal physician.

Other Endorsements:

My research company has investigated cancer and the cancer industry for over 12 years. During this time, we have had the opportunity to examine many alternative treatments for cancer in great detail. I do not hesitate to recommend Essiac products to the public as part of the metabolic therapy support program for the prevention of, and treatment for all types of cancer. Essiac is covered in my best-selling book, Cancer: Why We're Still Dying to Know the Truth, available through Credence Publications.
    Phillip Day
    Health Reporter

Credence Research, UK

Chapter 3. Kombucha the Amazing Mushroom Tea

Years ago the Russian government sent a team of investigators to check out why the residents of an area in Manchuria were cancer free. The people of this area also regularly lived to be over 100 years of age. After a two-year study, the investigators attributed the longevity and good health of these people to a yeast enzyme tea called Kombucha. It had been part of their diet for hundreds of years. Now the use of Kombucha has been spreading like wildfire in the United States.

In an April, 1995 issue of US Today newspaper, an article about Kombucha tea stated that five to six million Americans were drinking Kombucha tea daily. I am sure that this number of Kombucha drinkers has grown since then. It is inexpensive, I find it fun to make, and most people enjoy the taste. I keep several one gallon "sun tea" jars of Kombucha brewing at all times. I keep the jars prominently sitting on my kitchen counter, where they become a conversation piece for my visitors.

During an August, 1995 TV program of Entertainment Tonight which covered Kombucha, it was mentioned that the Hollywood stars Cher, Susan Sarandon, Martin Landau, Meg Ryan and Linda Evans were all Kombucha drinkers. In addition, Anjelica Huston, Lily Tomlin, Morgan Fairchild, and Rita Coolidge are said to be Kombucha fans. It is reported that Kombucha cleanses the blood, stops cancer, increases energy levels, reverses hardening of the arteries, reduces high blood pressure, boosts T-cell counts, removes wrinkles, thickens the hair, and relieves headaches. Studies in California report that HIV patients drinking Kombucha do not progress into AIDS. Other testimonials state that it reverses graying hair, stops PMS, reverses the symptoms of multiple sclerosis, and shrinks prostates.

Kombucha is known to provide the liver with glucuronic acid, a substance that the liver uses to detoxify our bodies. In this manner, Kombucha helps the liver to perform its critical function of "binding up" toxic substances so they can be carried away by the blood and dispelled from our bodies.

Amazom.com on the Internet sells a number of books about Kombucha. There is also the book "***Kombucha: Healthy Beverage and Natural Remedy from the Far East***" by Guenther Frank which can be purchased from Pronatura, Inc. at 847-545-1003.

Kombucha has been around for centuries without causing any known widespread ill effects. Although newly discovered in the United States, there has been plentiful research done in Europe and Asia confirming its healthful benefits. Kombucha is fun to make, tastes great, is cheap, and if you take it daily, you too may live to become 100 years old.

Sources of a Kombucha Starter Kit

1. Mt. Nebo Herbs & Oils, 300 Highland Ave., Athens OH 45701, Tel: 740-592-3795 sells a Kombucha starter kit, including Kombucha mushroom and full instructions for $15.50 plus $6.95 for Shipping.

2. 2. Laurel Farms, PO Box 2896, Sarasota FL 34230, Tel: 941-351-2233 sells a Kombucha starter kit, including Kombucha mushroom and full instructions, for $39.00 including Shipping and Handling.

3. Nancy Adams, Ph.D., Tel: 541-888-5111, sells a Kombucha starter kit for $15.00 including Shipping.

Note: These starter kits are all that you will need to produce a lifetime supply of Kombucha tea.

Chapter 4. Pycnogenol and Grape Seed Extract

An excess of free radicals in a person's body causes major damage, including cancer. Free radicals can attack, damage, and ultimately destroy any material including the sensitive cells and tissues in the body. The best free radical killer is Pycnogenol (pronounced pig-nodge-a-nol). Pycnogenol is a patented antioxidant from France that is made from a pine tree bark extract.

Let's talk more about free radicals. The normal oxygen atom in your body has four pairs of electrons. However the effects of radiation, sunlight, air pollution, harmful chemicals, food additives, tobacco smoke, infections and stress can rob one of the electrons from the oxygen atom. This atom is now a free radical. It tries to replace its lost electron by raiding other molecules. It will rob an electron from a molecule in a cell wall. This robbed molecule proceeds to replace its lost electron by robbing another molecule, and a chain reaction is created. This leads to disintegration of the cell, and opens the door to cancer and many other ills. It also alters the DNA which damages the way in which the cells in your body replicate. This leads to aging. Some studies suggest that these free radicals are a major cause of aging.

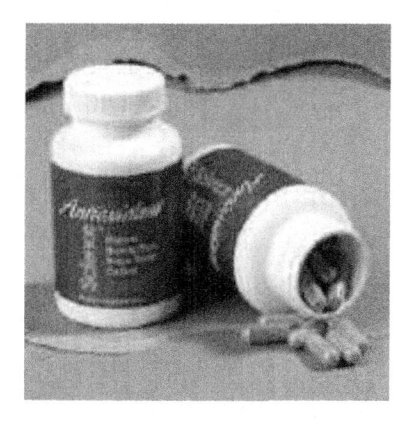

How does Pycnogenol help? It is a very powerful antioxidant. An antioxidant has extra electrons that it can "give up" to the free radicals, thereby rendering them harmless.

I recommend Pycnogenol because of its power. It has the ability, in a matter of a few months, to destroy all of the excess free radicals that you have built up over a lifetime. It is inexpensive. It is easy to locate. It comes in tablet form. Every health food store stocks it. Dr. Lamar Rosquist recommends that you take one mg. of Pycnogenol daily per pound of body weight during the initial period when you are ridding yourself of all accumulated free radicals. This means that a 200 pound man would take 200 mg. of Pycnogenol daily for the first two or three months. Later you may wish to slack off to a lower maintenance-level dosage.

Pycnogenol is reported to assist in the recovery of cancer, Alzheimers, arthritis, Parkinsons, rheumatism, asthma, diabetes, stress, varicose veins, phlebitis, PMS, AIDS, senility, M.S., chronic fatigue, stroke, circulatory and cardiovascular problems. It adds energy. It has also been reported to greatly assist in limiting wrinkling and aging of the skin.

When I took Pycnogenol, I found my energy levels dramatically boosted.

Grape Seed Extract is reportedly as good as Pycnogenol as a free radical killer. To locate a source of Pycnogenol or Grape Seed Extract, I suggest that you visit one or more health food stores. They may be able to offer some helpful advice, and they may have literature available with additional information about this antioxidant. I have even found Pycnogenol and Grape Seed Extract stocked in K Mart and my local drug store.

Sources of Pycnogenol and Grape Seed Extract

Nature's Rx, 119 Spinnaker Circle, Madison AL 35758, Toll Free Tel: 800-303-5781 sells Grape Seed Extract. A bottle of 90 caplets (90mg per cap) costs $12.00.

Nutri Team, Ripton VT 05766, Toll Free Tel: 800-785-9791 sells Grape Seed Extract. A bottle of 120 caplets (100 mg per cap) costs $11.95.

Primary Source, Inc., PO Box 812, Fairfield CT 06430, Toll Free Tel: 888-666-1188 sells a product named OPC that contains both Pycnogenol and grape seed extract. A bottle of 60 caplets (100 mg per cap) costs $44.95.

Chapter 5. Colon Health and Cancer

Almost everyone remembers that John Wayne died of cancer. When an autopsy was performed on him, it was found that his colon (large intestine) was six inches in diameter and weighed 60 pounds empty. The hole in the center of the colon through which his food passed was one inch in diameter. The large intestine of the average person is about 5 feet long, and is 2.5 inches in diameter. John Wayne's enlarged colon was so packed with an accumulation of undigested and solidified food that there was no way in which he could have lived. I say that John Wayne died of an unhealthy colon, because cancer is only one of the results of an unhealthy and blocked colon.

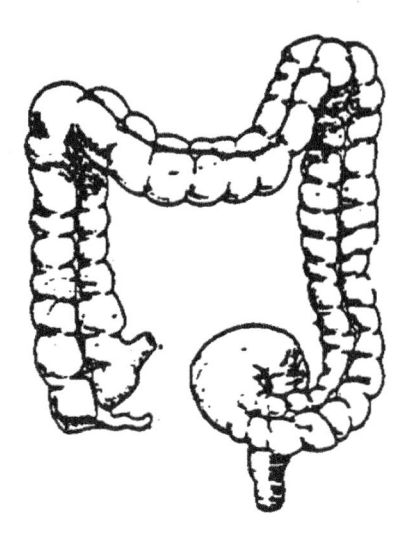

One of the functions of the blood in your body is to carry oxygen and nutrients to each cell in your body. The blood, after delivering this oxygen and nutrition to each cell, then picks up the waste product of the cell and carries it to the wall of the colon. There the waste products are passed through the wall of the colon, to be carried out of the body with the next bowel movement. However, if the interior walls of the colon have become coated with solidified food and waste, this coating on the wall of the colon will block the passage of the blood's load of waste products. Thus, this function of passing the blood's load of cell waste cannot be performed. The blood, not able to unload its load of waste products, will begin to carry it around the body. Loaded down with this load of toxic waste products, the blood is not able to pick up a full load of oxygen and nutrients to resupply the body's cells. Starved of the necessary oxygen and nutrients, the body's cells begin to deteriorate. This leads to a host of unhealthy conditions, including eventually cancer. Remember, in Chapter 1 we discussed that cancer can only exist in an environment where there is a lack of oxygen. So it is that the state of health of your large intestine (colon) has a lot to do with whether or not you get cancer.

It is a medical fact that
the average American male has a coating of solidified food lining the inside walls of his colon which weighs five pounds! How does this happen? A lifetime of eating too many fatty foods, a diet not containing enough fiber, and too many processed foods in our diet are the culprits. The eventual result of our years of improper eating is that deposits begin to accumulate on the walls of the colon, eventually leading to serious health situations, as emphasized by the example of John Wayne.

Symptoms of an Unhealthy Colon

As we get older, we begin to experience the symptoms of aging. But many times, these are not the symptoms of the normal aging process, they are symptoms of a plugged up colon. We just mistake them as signs of the normal aging process. Symptoms of an unhealthy colon are:

Fatigue	Depression	Anxiety or worry
Gas or Flatulence	Protruding Abdomen	Insomnia
Not feeling good	Lack of interest	Abdominal discomfort
Headaches	Aches and pains	Menstrual problems
Irritability	Loss of memory	Skin problems
Nervousness	Overweight	Bad breath
Nausea	Craving for food	Feel cold (hands and feet)
Swelling of the legs	Disinterest in sex	

What Can Be Done?

Obviously, changing your diet to minimize fats and processed foods, and adding fiber, will be required in order to correct the conditions of an unhealthy colon. But if you have cancer, you cannot afford to wait for the months or years it may take to correct the problem. You need to fix your colon now. The answer is Colonics.

What is a Colonic?

A Colonic is much like an enema, except that it is much more thorough and effective. In a 45-minute session, approximately 15 gallons of water is used to gently flush the colon. Through appropriate use of massage, pressure points, etc., the colon therapist is able to work loose and eliminate far more toxic waste than any other short-term technique.

Colonics and your colon

Specifically, a Colonic is used to accomplish the following:

1. It cleanses the Colon: Toxic material is broken down so it can no longer harm your body or inhibit assimilation and elimination. Even debris built up over a long period is gently, but surely removed in the process of a series of treatments. Once impacted material is removed, your colon can begin again to co-operate as it was intended to. In this very real sense a colonic is a rejuvenation treatment.

2. It Exercises the Colon Muscles: The build up of toxic debris weakens the colon and impairs it's functioning. The gentle filling and emptying of the colon improves peristaltic (muscular contraction) activity by which the colon naturally moves material.

3. It Reshapes the Colon: When problem conditions exist in the colon, they tend to alter its shape which in turn causes more problems. The gentle action of the water, coupled with the massage techniques of the colon therapist helps to eliminate bulging pockets of waste and narrowed, spastic constrictions. This enables the colon to resume its natural state.

4. It Stimulates Reflex Points: Every system and organ of the body is connected to the colon by reflex points. A colonic stimulates these points, thereby affecting the corresponding body parts in a beneficial way.

When the lower intestinal tract is cleansed, the whole system is detoxified. Proponents of colon irrigation claim that it actually heals their bodies. Toxicity is a major cause of illness, disease and feelings of general malaise. While colon therapy does not heal any specific disease, it greatly enhances the body's ability to function at optimum levels, so the body is more able to heal itself.

When a system has experienced abusive treatment it has had to endure over a lifetime, toxic waste builds up in the colon and the body cannot properly assimilate the vitamins and minerals we need. The walls of the colon tend to develop a buildup of material and this results in sluggish bowel movements, constipation and other problems. Instead of being expelled correctly, the poisons re-enter the blood stream and circulate through the body. If you are experiencing flatulence, stomach bloat, lower backache, bad breath, stiff joints, mood swings, skin problems, abdominal discomfort, restless sleep, excessive mucous, nausea, constipation, diarrhea, fatigue depression or cloudy urine, you may need to have your colon cleansed. These are signs of an impacted colon.

Many people are under the false impression that an enema is as cleansing as a colonic. An enema only uses 1 to 2 quarts of water while colonic irrigation uses 12 to 15 gallons of water. During the colonic the water travels the whole 5-foot length of the colon, cleaning it from the sigmoid to the ascending colon. The whole colonic treatment is not necessarily limited to the colonic irrigation. Also included usually is abdominal massage and reflexology that is used to stimulate pressure points of the feet that also help with the elimination process. The entire procedure should take 35 to 40 minutes.

The effect of a colonic is not just on the colon. Once your body is detoxified through the colonic irrigation, the other organs of the body work better. It facilitates the cleansing of the blood, liver and the lymphatic system

and makes it easier for organs to release their waste products for elimination. Many people claim they suffer from headaches much less after having a colonic treatment. Other benefits that are reported are improvement in appearance, mental attitude, skin tone, and stress is relieved.
Constipation and abdominal pain are often eliminated and the old feeling of exhaustion is replaced with a feeling of energy. And if you have cancer, the glands and organs of your body will function better, causing your immune system to work better, and be able to better combat the cancer in your body.

Where Can I Get a Colonic?

Good places to locate a colon therapist who will administer a colonic are your local health food store bulletin board and the telephone book yellow pages. You may also wish to ask about among the health-conscious. One of them will be able to recommend a good colonics specialist to you.

Chapter 6. Cancer and the Parasite Connection

Dr Hulda Clark is a medical researcher from Canada. She is convinced that many diseases, especially cancer, result from the invasion of parasites in the colon.

Dr. Hulda Clark

From this simply stated but well researched idea, she has written a series of books and produced a range of products and recommendations which have resulted in a huge following in the United States of America and in many other countries.

Her first best selling book " The Cure for all Cancers" has been followed by "The Cure for all Diseases", and she has developed her ideas and her following by the good results her patients are experiencing. Dr Clark believes that if the body can be rid of colon parasites it can restore itself to full health. Dr Clark recommends a combination of herbal parasite cleanses, the use of her inexpensive electronic "zapper", and kidney and liver flushes as the best possible ways to rid the body of colon parasites.

How is it that a parasite can cause cancer?

Unknown to most of us, most people have one or more types of parasites in their bodies. They got them from running barefoot as children, from eating undercooked meat, from eating improperly washed fruits and vegetables, and from handling pets. One of these parasites is an intestinal fluke. Its scientific name is

Fasciolopsis buskli. It is quite small. Normally this fluke lives in our intestinal tract, where it does little harm. But sometimes, over years without detection or treatment, these flukes multiply to the point where they begin to travel outside the colon to other parts of the body. Sometimes they invade other organs or parts of the body. There they do a great deal of harm. There they can cause cancer.

For example, let us assume a situation where these intestinal flukes have invaded and established themselves in a liver. There they multiply until there may be thousands of flukes. These flukes are all busy devouring your body fluids and nutrients, and in turn spewing out their waste products. These waste products contaminate your liver. There is a growth factor in your liver that is called ortho-phospo-tyrosine. For brevity I shall refer to it as "ortho". This ortho has a normal function of causing cells to divide. But the fluke's waste products cause the ortho to sometimes go haywire, and the ortho causes cells to divide where they shouldn't. This leads to improperly growing cells, which often leads to cancer.

Why Cancer Locates Where It Does

Why does one person develop cancer in the lungs, and another person develop cancer in the kidneys? It is because this particular area of the body is weakened. Generally, parasites thrive better in a weakened organism. So the flukes will be attracted to this weakened area of the body. Eventually a cancerous condition will develop.

Why is this particular part of the body weakened? Because it probably has a number of the following problems:

a. has low immune power
b. accumulated a heavy dosage of heavy metals
c. accumulated a large dosage of toxins
d. receives improper nutrition
e. does not receive enough oxygen
f. has too many free radicals.

Let's Get Rid Of The Parasites!

Dr. Hulda Clark recommends the following protocols to get rid of the parasites in your body:

1. A Herbal Parasite Cleanse. Dr. Clark recommends a combination of Black Walnut Hull extract, Wormwood and Cloves. My favorite source for these parasite-removing products is the company founded by Hanna Kroeger, a famous herbalist. It is Kroeger Herbal Products, 805 Walnut St., Boulder CO 80302, Toll Free Tel: 800-516-0690. Tell them what you wish to do, and they will advise which products to buy and how to take them. They are very honest people.
2. The "Zapper". Dr Clark discovered that a minute electrical charge, at a certain frequency, will kill all of the parasites without harming the body. She has developed an inexpensive device named the "Zapper" which will do this. She provides complete construction details and schematics in her book *The Cure For All Cancers*. All parts can be bought at Radio Shack. However if you are as electronically illiterate as I am, I

suggest that you buy a Zapper from one of the many small companies that supply them to the public. You may wish to call:
   a. Essence Instruments, 119 Pearl St., Kingston NY 12401, Toll Free Tel: 877-317-3341. Cost is $65.00
   b. Transformation Technologies, PO Box 2698, North Hills CA 91393, Toll Free Tel: 877-287-0712. Cost is $80.00
   c. Sota Instruments, PO Box 2698, Revelstoke BC, Canada, North America Toll Free Tel: 800-224-0242. Cost is $83.00.
3. Liver and Kidney Flushes. She also gives detailed instructions in her book on how to give yourself a liver and kidney flush. I have done these flushes on a number of occasions. They cost almost nothing, take only a day, and give only the mildest discomfort. In short, they are a breeze. You will feel in much better health after taking them.

The Book

If this parasite information is of interest to you, you definitely should take the plunge and buy the book **The Cure For All Cancers** by Dr. Hulda Clark, MD. The normal retail price is $21.95. If your local health food store does not stock the book, you can order it at .ww.amazon.com, or you may contact Spirit of Healing, 144 N. Cherry St, #7, Kernersville NC 27284, Toll Free Tel: 877-275-3196.

Other Doctor's Comments

"It is Dr. Clark's merit to have discovered the fact that parasitic burdens play a central role in cancer." -- Dr. Alan Baklayan, Orthomolecular Medicine, Munich, Germany

"We have a tremendous parasite problem right here in the United States-it's just not being identified."
-Peter Weina, Ph.D., Chief of Pathobiology, Walter Reed Army Institute of Research, 1991

"I strongly believe that every patient with disorders of immune function, including multiple allergies (especially food allergy), and patients with unexplained fatigue or with chronic bowel symptoms should be evaluated for the presence of intestinal parasites."
-Leo Galland, M.D. Townsend Letter for Doctors, 1988

"Make no mistake about it, worms are the most toxic agents in the human body. They are one of the primary underlying causes of disease and are the most basic cause of a compromised immune system."
-Hazel Parcells, D.C., N.D., Ph.D., 1974

Testimonials

Cancer Testimonial #1

On October 8, 1998, at age 55, I was diagnosed with cutaneous T Cell Lymphoma. I was given a few months to live. A bone marrow was done and a catscan was taken four days later, coincident with the commencement of chemotherapy. A week later, the results of the bone marrow and catscan indicated a more promising prognosis -- I could live another five years. Five months of chemotherapy ensued.

At the end of the chemotherapy (February), my oncologist and I were pleased with the results. Chemo was done! He would see me again in three months.

Unfortunately in mid April, the lymphoma returned. The largest tumor was removed but two more tumors grew. The doctors felt that neither chemo nor surgery would work so they decided to try radiation. In Canada, we have a waiting period to try radiation so it was booked for July.

I was terrified of having radiation and decided to pursue Hulda Clark's book, the Cure for All Cancers, which I had bought during my chemotherapy sessions. Commencing with the daily kidney cleanse tea, and then adding the parasite cleanse, I followed the regimen in her book. Three weeks later, the tumors were gone!

On July 7, I met with the radiologist as it was a consultation only. He examined me and said, you don't need radiation, you look great. He also confirmed that radiation, as it is a 'spot' treatment, would not get all the cancer, only certain tumors. He was very interested in the cleanses I was taking and researched the ingredients while I was at the hospital. His conclusion was they were doing me no harm, in fact 'wormwood' is known in medical circles to kill tumors and advised he would render a report to my oncologist. The radiologist recommended a kidney test to ensure the cleanse was not toxic to my kidneys; however, he felt the dose was too minimal to be toxic.

August 9, I saw my oncologist and after several blood and kidney tests, was told I did not need to see him again, I could expect to live a 'normal life expectancy', I was fine! We have jointly agreed to checkups every 3 months as a preventative measure. Interestingly, I showed him a bottle of the parasite cleanse and he said I was the second of his patients to show him the cleanse, the other patient had leukemia, and was doing as well as I.

October 2, I returned from two weeks, touring, hiking and exploring the Canadian Rockies. I feel great, thanks to Hulda Clark.

I realize that testimonials can be 'a dime a dozen' but having been diagnosed with what we all dread, Cancer, I decided early in my diagnosis that I had to take control of my healing and exhaust all opportunities -- dying was never on my agenda. What did I have to lose, nothing and I had my life to gain. My two daughters thought I was crazy to do the cleanse but support it wholeheartedly now. There are many of us taking the cleanse and doing well, some who have refused all 'conventional medical' treatment (chemotherapy and radiation).

I think I owe my life to Hulda Clark's parasite cleanse.

Sincerely,
CT

Cancer Testimonial #2

We just received the great news that JL is cured of cancer! You might remember her -- she is 30 years of age and was suffering from Stage 3 brain cancer. Chemo was failing her since there was new growth after the chemo treatments. She has written you and was closely following the parasite cleanse and using the zapper. She went to a local clinic for a body scan and she was told that he couldn't pick up any evidence that she had cancer. Therefore, she had her M.D. schedule a special test in Phoenix in hopes that the medical community would agree with the alternative therapist. Sure enough, results just came back that the growth of her tumor was not only retarded but she showed no evidence of any tumor at all! Needless to say, she and her family have received the best Christmas present ever.

Please send our thanks to Dr. Clark. She has touched another desperately ill person.

JG

Cancer Testimonial #3

I am writing to tell our my story, which is not as dramatic as some, but VERY important to me. I had just begun reading Dr. Clark's "A Cure for All Diseases" because a friend had been diagnosed with cancer. At about that same time, my mammogram showed a highly suspicious growth. My doctor recommended an immediate biopsy, but I decided to give Dr. Clark's protocol a try first. Within 3 weeks, the lump was completely gone, and there has been no trace for 2 yrs. All of this is documented in my medical records.

Just as importantly, by reading Dr. Clark's book, I became aware of things I was using and consuming that contributed to my body's workload. I am a health conscious health care provider, but there were many things I learned about even "health store products"... As a result, I have changed my life, and my health. I continue with Dr. Clark's maintenance protocol, and will do so for the rest of my life. We now make our own soaps, lotions, and shampoos. We use many of Dr. Clark's recipes since she had supplied alternatives to everyday products. I try to look at everything we use and consume through Dr. Clark's eyes.

C.C.

Chapter 7. MGN-3

The development of the product known as MGN-3 is relatively new in the field of alternative medicine. But it has exciting promise as a cancer fighter.

There are more than 130 subtypes of white blood cells that make up the immune system. The most important are the T, B, and NK cells. T and B cells are responsible for producing antibodies and chemical messengers (cytokines) that mobilize the immune system for action, while NK cells make up the body's first line of defense. The key to optimum immune system function appears to be not the raw number of NK cells (most people have them in adequate numbers), but the number and activity of the microscopic granules within each NK cell.

By encouraging the development of large numbers of highly active granules within the NK cells, MGN-3 works to "tune up" the immune system while optimizing T, B, and NK cell function.

MGN-3 is manufactured using a patented

process that hydrolyzes rice bran with the enzymatic extract of shiitake mushrooms. In published studies, MGN-3 was shown to increase NK cell activity by more than 300%, B cell activity by 250% or greater, and T cell activity by 200% . This is better results than are obtained with any other vitamin, herbal or medicinal mushroom therapies.

Stimulating these immune system cells with MGN-3 gives the immune system the ammunition it needs to keep the entire body in good health.

Sources of MGN-3

1. Better Health International, 2025 Oakland Ave., Indiana PA 15701, Toll Free Tel: 800-772-5568. $39.95 for 50 capsules, 250 mg. each.
2. American Nutrition, 5092 Buttercup Dr., Castle Rock CO 80104, Toll Free

Tel: 800-454-3724. $43.50 for 50 capsules, 250 mg. each.
3. Brower Enterprises, 102 S Main St., Canton SD 57013, Toll Free Tel" 800-373-6076. $49.00 for 50 capsules, 250 mg. each.

Research Information on MGN-3

Following is excerpted information from several prominent research reports about MGN-3. Although a bit technical in nature, these reports are worth reviewing. Basically, they confirm that MGN-3 works!

Research Report #1

Report by: Uyemura, Koichi; Tarchiki, Ken; Ghoneurn, Mamdooh; Makinodan, Takashi; Makhijani Nalini; Yamaguchi, Dean of UCLA Medical School/Greater Los Angeles VA Healthcare System, Los Angeles CA; Drew University of Medicine and Science, Los Angeles CA and UCLA School of Medicine/Greater Los Angeles VA Healthcare System, Los Angeles CA

There is great interest among health care professionals to explore the value of naturally derived biological response modifiers to enhance immune function. MGN-3 is a biological response modifier that is an arabinoxylan compound which is a polysaccharide containing hemicellulose-b extract of rice bran, modified by enzymes from Shiitake mushrooms reported previously to be a potent immunomodulator. We have previously shown that treatment with MGN-3 had an augmentory effect on natural killer [NK] cell activity in healthy control subjects, in patients with breast cancer, and in patients infected with HIV-1. In these studies, an effect on NK cell activity was noted as early as 4 weeks and did not show hyporesponsiveness with continued treatment for over 12 months, with absence of notable side effects. In the present study, we demonstrate a direct effect of MGN-3 on tumor cell growth and cytokine production. Preliminary results showed that incubation of a breast cancer cell line (MCF-7) with MGN-3 arrested tumor cell growth, whereas control MCF-12A cells grown in a media in the absence of added MGN-3 continued to increase in cell number. Employing flow cytometry procedures, results showed that after 16 hours of treatment of MCF-7 cells with MGN-3 showed a marked stimulation in production of interleukin 10 {IL- 10}. ELISA analyses of the culture media bathing the cells 16 hours after treatment with MGN-3 also showed an increase in IL-10 production, little change in INF-g concentration. However, a marked elevation in Interlukin-12 was also observed at 16 hours. **In conclusion, our findings indicate that MGN-3 acts by not only enhancing the activity of NK cells as previously reported, but also through a direct action on tumor cell production of cytokines.** The production of cytokines such as IL-10 by cancer cells to alter the activity of the immune system is well known. Our findings indicate that the biological response modifier MGN-3 can alter the production and secretion of cytokines such as IL-10 and IL-12 by cancer cells such as MCF-7; and thereby the activity of the immune system. Findings that treatment of cultures of MCF-7 cells with MGN-3 also can arrest cell growth directly may reflect an alternate mechanism of control of tumor cell growth. MGN-3, commercially known as Biobran, was provided by Daiwa Pharmaceuticals

Company, Ltd. Tokyo, Japan. Work in this direction is in progress. Supported in part by VA Medical Research Funds and by funds provided by Daiwa Pharmaceuticals Company, Ltd, Tokyo, Japan

MUSHROOM AMMUNITION
© ALTERNATIVE MEDICINE DIGEST, MAY 1999

Dr. Mamdooh Ghoneum of Charles Drew University of Medicine and Science in Los Angeles compares current cancer treatment to battling terrorists. By bombing a city, you can kill most terrorists, although innocent civilians will also be killed. "Chemotherapy, radiation or surgery are the cancer-equivalents of bombing," he says, "and the beneficial white blood cells in the area are non-terrorist victims." Even after bombing, however, some terrorists may survive, as do those cancer cells that are resistant to the usual therapies. Rather than bombing the city again, however, Dr. Ghoneum advocates sending in Special Forces to locate and eliminate the remaining terrorists one by one.

Dr. Ghoneum's development of a natural supplement called MGN-3 is meant to arm the body's Natural Killer cells to seek and destroy dangerous invaders one by one. The human immune system is comprised of more than 130 subsets of white blood cells. About 15% of them are called Natural Killer (NK) cells. These provide the first line of defense for dealing with any form of invasion to the body. Each cell contains several small granules which act as 'ammunition.' When an NK cell recognizes a cancer cell, for instance, it attaches itself to the cell's outer membrane and injects these granules directly into the interior of the cell. The granules then 'explode,' destroying the cancer cell within five minutes. The killer cell then moves on to other cancer cells and repeats the process. As long as NK cells remain active, the body is able to keep disease under control.

The supplement developed by Dr. Ghoneum, called MGN-3, increases the efficacy of the NK cells. Additionally, it has other immune-boosting effects as well: it increases levels of interferon, a compound produced by the body that inhibits the replication of viruses; it increases the formation of Tumor Necrosis Factors, a group of proteins that help destroy cancer cells; and it increases the activity of T-cells and B-cells. This potent immune system booster is made of the outer shell of rice bran which has been enzymatically treated with extracts from the medicinal Shiitake mushroom. In Japan, mushroom extracts have become the leading prescription treatments for cancer. Dr. Ghoneum's findings have been demonstrated in test-tube experiments as well as seven published studies involving 72 patients. In a study presented to the American Association for Cancer Research, he reported on five patients with breast cancer. Each patient was treated with the same dosage of three grams a day of MGN-3 from a Japanese manufacturer. NK cell activity increased within two weeks and continued to do so as the study progressed. At the end of the six- to eight-month study, two of the patients were in complete remission. In a study reported the following year, 27 patients with various types of cancers including breast, cervical, prostate, leukemia and multiple myeloma were tested for NK cell activity by 51 Chromium release assay before and after only two weeks treatment with MGN-3. NK cell activity increased 154-332% for breast carcinoma, 100-275% in cervical cancer, 174-385% in prostatic cancer, 100-240% in leukemia and 100-537% in multiple myeloma.

One multiple myeloma patient was a 58-year-old man diagnosed in 1990. He underwent several months of chemotherapy following his diagnosis. Although his condition seemed to stabilize, his blood still showed markers for multiple myeloma eight months after chemotherapy. He then began taking MGN-3 and in less than 6 months, follow-up lab work showed no indication of cancer. Today eight years after his initial diagnosis, he is the first patient known to have survived multiple myeloma, according to Dr. Ghoneum.

Dr. Warren Levin, 66, a holistic physician practicing in New York City and Ridgefield, Connecticut, had suffered from an immune deficiency with an abnormal ratio of helper cells to suppressor cells since the early '80s. "I tried herbs, healers, intravenous treatments, all sorts of stuff. Several years ago, I learned about glyconutrients — carbohydrate molecules that play a critically important role in cell-to-cell communication. I began looking for glyconutrient sources. All over the world, native populations were using substances with high glyconutrient content including Aloe Vera, astralagus, echinacea and various mushrooms. At that point, I read an article about MGN-3. I was already taking Coats Aloe Vera Concentrate together with Beta 1-3, D-glucan (Macroforce), Ambrotose, and a thymus preparation called Basic Thymic Protein A as well as the usual vitamins, minerals and antioxidants. I also did intensive mercury detoxification with DMPS. Last fall, I began taking six capsules a day of MGN-3. At the end of December, I sent my blood to the laboratory and when I returned from vacation I found that for the first time in 15 years, every one of my tests had improved well into the middle range of normalcy. That combination of supplements had finally reversed my helper-cell ratio. And normalized my mitogen/allergen responses and NK cell activity."

Dr. Ghoneum's latest study, reported in the International Journal of Immunotherapy, involved 24 patients. Doctors tested NK cell activity in each patient, administered the recommended cancer dosage of 3 grams per day, and tested NK cell activity again after 16 hours, one week, one month and two months. After 16 hours NK cell activity had increased 1.3 to 1.5 times. After one week, activity had increased eightfold. **At the end of two months, NK cells were killing 27 times more cancer cells than prior to taking MGN-3.**

Unlike other forms of cancer treatment, MGN-3 is a totally harmless substance and has no known side effects. In the terrorist analogy, it doesn't kill innocent civilians. David A. Pitts, 73, a real estate salesman in Santa Barbara, California, had undergone chemotherapy for lymphoma treatments with no apparent results. "I had been getting weaker and weaker," he said. After a report on MGN-3, he sent for the supplement and began taking it while he was also placed on a course of intravenous treatment with trioxine, a relatively new drug. "In about three to four weeks on the outside, gosh, I started feeling better," says Pitts. "What really intrigued me was the idea that this supplement could enhance your immune system. When I began, I did a crash program of 14 capsules a day. Now I'm on a preventative program of four a day." At his latest CAT-scan, Pitts was in remission. "The doctor had no explanation of how or why this happened, and there's nothing I can prove. But I'm going to continue taking this for the rest of my life. What's in it is harmless and doesn't interfere with anything else."

Dr. Ghoneum has also used MGN-3 to treat hepatitis B and C and has done in vitro experiments demonstrating its action against HIV. He believes that individuals in "high risk" categories for disease can benefit from using MGN-3 preventively. These include:

- Heavy smokers
- Heavy drinkers
- Individuals, such as artists and house

painters, who constantly work with paint
- Those born with immune deficiencies
- Families with a strong history of cancer
- Chemical and refinery workers

Research Report #3

Associate Professor and Chief of Research, Department of Otolaryngology, Charles D. Drew University; Research Associate, Department of Neurobiology, UCLA School of Medicine

Background:

Although cynicism and disillusionment with the failed "war against cancer" are widespread, I remain very optimistic that we will triumph over this seemingly invincible killer. Given the disappointing results and many drawbacks of cytotoxic therapies, it seems clear that our best hope for a decisive victory against cancer lies in immuno-augmentive therapies, those that enhance the body's innate immune response to cancer cells.

As a research immunologist, I have spent 18 years studying immunomodulating substances — natural compounds derived from mushrooms, herbs, fungi, and bacteria, as well as synthetic drugs like Interleukin-2 and Interferon. Approximately six years ago, I stumbled across a natural substance that was so promising, so profoundly superior to everything else I had ever evaluated, that I abandoned all other projects, including NIH-funded research, in order to focus entirely on this substance. The product, MGN-3 (an arabinoxylane compound), is a polysaccharide composed of the hemicellose-ß extract of rice bran, modified by enzymes from Shiitake mushrooms. As we have detailed in 7 previously published studies, involving a total of 72 human subjects, the efficacy of MGN-3 equals or surpasses the very best immune-modulating drugs available but, in stark contrast to these, exhibits a complete lack of toxicity.

(Copies of complete research papers and data on MGN-3 can be obtained from Lane Labs at 201-236-9090.)

Much of the data regarding MGN-3 has been previously published in technical journals and presented at international research conferences, but the information remains largely unknown to oncologists and other health professionals dealing directly with the cancer patient. The aim of this article is to bring this research to the attention of the practicing clinician, to summarize what is known about the actions of MGN-3, and explore its present role in the treatment of cancer patients.

Anti-viral activity:

In addition to very encouraging results using MGN-3 in the treatment of malignancies, other research suggests a promising role for MGN-3 as a therapy for HIV, Hepatitis C, and other viral infections. MGN-3 has antiviral activity and also enhances the body's immune response against virally infected cells. In vitro research shows that MGN-3 inhibits replication of the HIV virus without cytotoxicity in a dose-dependent manner. Human studies suggest that MGN-3 may also be extremely useful in the treatment of Hepatitis C. In these patients liver enzymes return to normal levels within 1-8 weeks of treatment with MGN-3. The results of our ongoing clinical research into the antiviral applications of MGN-3 will be the subject of future reports.

The role of NK cells in the treatment of cancer:

Over 150 different types of white blood cells have been identified and, of these, NK cells are one of the most common, representing up to 15% of total white blood cells. They are important because, unlike other white blood cells, they are able to work more or less independently, not requiring special instructions from the immune system in order to recognize or attack a foreign cell. For this reason, they are often considered to be the body's first line of defense against cancer and viral-infected cells. Circulating through the body by way of the blood and lymph systems, the majority of NK cells present in the body are in a resting state. NK cells become more active in response to immunoregulatory proteins called cytokines. Once activated, the NK cells become quite rapacious in their search-and-destroy activities. Upon encountering a tumor cell, the activated NK cell attaches to the membrane of the cancer cell and injects cytoplasmic granules that quickly dissolve (lyse) the target cell. In less than five minutes, the cancer cell is dead and the NK moves on to its next victim. **A single NK cell can destroy up to 27 cancer cells before it dies. Although quite small in comparison to tumor or virus cells, a single NK cell can often bind to two or more cancer cells at once.**

The absolute number of NK cells present in the blood gives little indication of the efficiency of immune function. Instead, it is the activity of the NK cells — the avidity with which they recognize and bind to tumor cells — that is important. Most immunomodulators, including MGN-3, do not increase the number or percentage of NK cells, but instead increase their level of activation. NK cell activity can be tested by means of a 4-hour radioactive-Chromium release assay. NK cells are isolated from a blood sample and are incubated in vitro with a fixed number of chromium-labeled tumor cells. After 4 hours, the percentage of tumor cells that have been killed by the NK cells is determined, and this percentage can be used to describe NK cell activity.

In a healthy immuno-competent individual, when NK cell activity is examined at an effector:target ratio of 100:1, we would expect to see NK cell activity ranging from 60-75%. However, in cancer patients, NK cell activity typically ranges from near 0% to 30%. Although it is not entirely clear whether this is a cause or result of the disease process, there is evidence suggesting that low NK cell activity may be a risk factor for malignancy or metastases, as well as a negative prognostic indicator.

Chapter 8. Summary and Conclusion

Please remember that we are researchers, and not physicians. By all means check this information out with your doctor. What is especially attractive about most of these alternative medicine remedies is that they can many times be taken along with traditional medicine protocols. So, in a way, you can perhaps have your cake and eat it too; you can follow the regimen for your cancer that is prescribed by your doctor, and you can take some of these alternative therapies also. Ask your doctor about it.

There are too many alternative holistic therapies mentioned in this book to take all at once. So you may wish to rely on your own inner guidance and select a few to try out. Generally, most people report that only a few weeks are needed in order to tell if they are being helped. You should get some sort of indication that these therapies are working. It may be a greater sense of well-being, or signs of detoxification, or signs of lessened cancer activity. Trust your inner senses and guidance.

Reader Bonus!!!

Our Amazing Healing Discovery

In 2021 I made my most important healing discovery. I wish to share it with you. So here goes.

I began to study artificial intelligence. In reading up on the QFS (quantum financial system) that was just beginning to emerge in the banking system, I found some intriguing and hard-to-believe information. There was plenty of information available about what the QFS would do for mankind (better, faster banking, more honest and dependable system, etc.) there was little or no information about how it worked.

I have a personal rule; if I don't understand it, I avoid it. So I jumped into a quick study to see if I could understand it, since it seemed so important to the future of mankind.

Briefly, what I discovered is that as computers got more and more sophisticated, and faster and faster, and more "intelligent", scientists were reaching the point where they had learned how to interface computers with the human mind. I will not go any further in this explanation, because, frankly, it get freaky and hard-to-believe if you go any deeper.

As I was working my way through all of this, I got some advice in meditation. My spirit guides advised me not to fret because mankind had already been using this technology for a thousand years. They then mentioned the Holy Water used by the Catholic Church.

Years ago, when I practiced Radionics healing extensively, I had, yes, learned that Holy Water does have special healing power. I had actually bought some Holy Water online, placed it in test tube, and had used it as a "reagent" to speed up certain healing processes. In other words, when I added the vibrational qualities of the Holy Water to the vibrations that were being sent to a person's affliction, the healing process was improved. So I knew that Holy Water was special.

I next went to the Internet to learn more about Holy water. Here is how it is made; a group of Priests fill a church fountain or other container with water and then they pray over it. They, in essence, bless the water. Then it becomes Holy Water. Pretty simple.

There are 3 prayers that they may use for this process. All are basically the same. Here is one of them:

"Blessed are you, Lord, all-powerful God, who in Christ, the living water of salvation, blessed and transformed us. Grant that when we are sprinkled with this water or make use of it, we will be refreshed inwardly by the power of the Holy Spirit and continue to walk in the new life we received at Baptism."
I was surprised that the simplicity of this prayer. Basically, all it does is commit the water to the wonderful power of God. Then things got really wonderful and special. This is hard to explain, but I will try my best to explain it to you.

I was told that the water being blessed and prayed over was capable of assisting mankind much more. But it had to be instructed by God to do so. Then the water would directly (in the case of illness), attack and remove the illness. Or in case of emotional distress, remove the harmful emotions and restore the body to happiness and balance.

Basically, this process changes the water in your body from a passive status to a status where it becomes an active healing agent. It was emphatically stressed that, unless the water as asked by God to do this, it would not work.

Where an understanding of Artificial Intelligence comes in

If you ponder on this for a while, as I have done, things become more clear. Artificial Intelligence involves establishing a link with the human mind and a non-human object (the computer). This link goes through God. God somehow allows this link (information) to be passed on to other mechanisms in God's realm, and the work is done. Not a great explanation, but is the best that I can offer, given my own limitations.

Well, the same basic thing happens with Holy Water. I have explained this in other sections of my book "On Stormy Seas". The written works of Viktor Shauberger and Masaru Emoto also delve sufficiently to explain water's ability to carry conscience and intelligence.

Thus when the Priests pray over the water, they impart a request that God bless the water with their message. God does this, and from then on the water has special curative powers. The water then later passes this curative power on to you.

So my Spirit Guides are right. The enlightenment of our knowledge of artificial intelligence does lead us right back to the knowledge of Holy Water that has been known for a thousand years. Interesting.

Where are we going with this?

I have to be careful here, as I do not wish to inadvertently reveal anything that I am not supposed to reveal.

What my Spiritual Advisors have told me is to take the basic prayer to bless Holy Water and "soup it up" by asking the water to do extra things, which it will most probably be happy to do for you and God. Remember always that God is approving everything, so you cannot inadvertently ask for anything that goes against God's will. Should you accidently do so, it is simple. God will not grant your request.

So, my first chance to use this knowledge came when two of my beloved Essiac employees got sick from taking Covid vaccinations shots. They drank this water. They immediately got better. I have also been using this knowledge to improve my own health and well as helping my wife deal with some health issues. It is working for us. I am going to list here several of the requests that we have been using.

Dear God, Please instruct this water to remove all harmful substances from my body. Please remove all illness and disease from my body. Please remove all harm from the Covid and the Covid vaccinations. Thank you. We love you.	**Dear God, Please instruct the water in my body to restore my energy levels to that of a 35 year-old person. Thank you and I love you.**

Dear God, Please instruct this water to heal And cure the swelling in my feet And legs. Thank you. I love you.	Dear God, Please instruct this water to remove the excess and unhealthy fat from my body And restore my body shape to a healthy Condition. I love you. Thank you.

Using Energy Plates to assist us

Here is the system that I use; I use a credit card sized energy plate. I buy mine at purpleplates.com. These aluminum plates are imbued with life force energy. I have used them successfully for many years for other healing purposes. I then perform a consecration ritual where I pass the message for my healing to the energy plate, all the while asking God to approve everything. I then print the prayer request, cut it out, ask God to bless it (through a prayer) and tape it to the energy plate. I cover everything in plastic. I then take this energy plate and tape it or fasten it to the water pipe feeding the faucet where I draw my drinking and cooking water. Sometimes, depending on the complexity of the house water piping system, I just fasten the plate to the cold water line that feeds the house (usually near the water heater). Thus the blessed message is passed on to the water that I drink. The water does the rest. Some people prefer to carry the energy plate in their pocket. Either method works. After a while you may get your own inspiration on various ways to use this information. Just be sure to get God's permission.

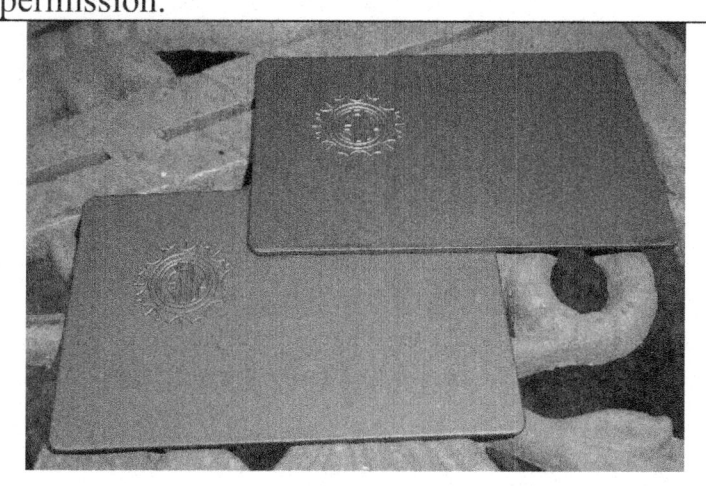

Energy plates (credit card size)

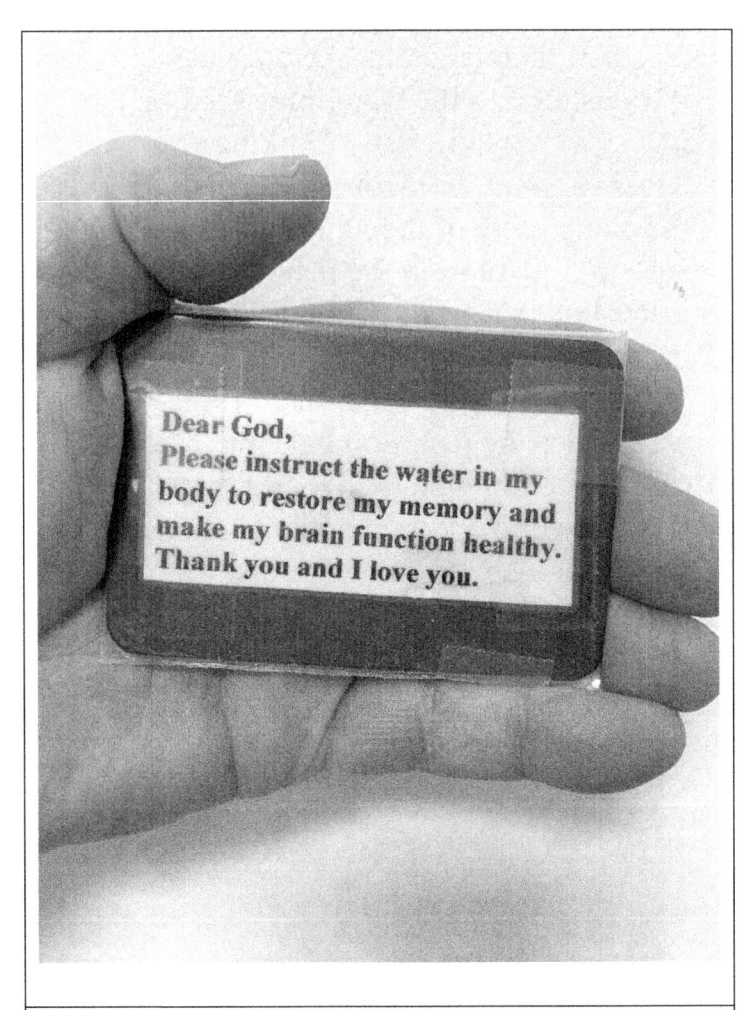

> Dear God,
> Please instruct the water in my body to restore my memory and make my brain function healthy. Thank you and I love you.

The finished product. Fasten to your water pipes. A sample prayer message is shown.